# Redefining Positive

## *How to Use Validation to Be a Positive Force in People's Lives*

Nicole Raheja

For information about special discounts available for bulk purchases, sales promotions, fund-raising, and educational needs, contact authorinquiries@nicoleraheja.com.

Cover design by Eli Dupree.

This book contains the opinions and ideas of its author. It is intended to provide helpful and informative material on the subjects addressed in the publication. It is sold with the understanding that the author is not engaged in rendering health, psychological, or any other kind of personal professional services in the book. The reader should consult a competent professional before adopting any of the suggestions in this book or drawing inferences from it. The author specifically disclaims all responsibility for any liability, loss, or risk, personal or otherwise, which is incurred as a consequence, directly or indirectly, of the use and application of any of the contents of this book.

*To Mom and Dad*

# Table of Contents

"I am no longer accepting the things I cannot change.
I am changing the things I cannot accept."
– Angela Davis

# Preface

When a friend is upset, our instinct can often be to cheer them up, or to help them look on the bright side of things. But there are times when a person needs to know that what they feel is valid. If you stepped onto my college campus, you would not believe that anyone could have had a bad experience there. Everyone you would have run into was friendly, outgoing, and cheerful, and you would rarely hear people complaining about their troubles. But going to college was one of the worst experiences of my life. Every day at college was miserable for me, to the point that I needed to leave my school. But whenever I expressed these feelings, people tried to convince me that my college was not actually that bad. Every step of the way, I was being encouraged to stick it out, and to think positively about things that were hurting me. College never improved for me – I was just as miserable at the end as I was in the beginning, and I regret putting myself through it. If I had had just one friend to tell me that my feelings were valid, I might have found the courage to leave.

What I learned from this experience is that being a good friend does not always mean smiling and looking on the bright side of things. It does not mean pushing people to be happy or have a positive attitude about things that are hurting them. Sometimes, being a positive force means accepting people's negative feelings and not pushing them to feel differently.

My college experience taught me just how much we need validation in our lives, and how so many of us never learned how to validate people's feelings. Validation is not something that we all learn as children, but it should be. I realized that I needed to write this book in order to help people learn to validate, so that maybe the next time someone is in a situation like I was in, they will get the validation that they need.

This book is experience-based. I have gone through many instances in my life where I didn't get the support I needed, or when I didn't give someone else the support that they needed, and figured out what could have been done differently. I am not a mental health professional, but I hope that I can use my experience to make things better going forward.

In this book, I will show you how to validate people's feelings. I use a variety of examples from different stages of life, including school, work, and personal settings. This book includes detailed examples of people having their feelings invalidated, which may be upsetting to read. Content warnings are included for the specific issues of abuse, sexual assault, and body image. In the stories that I share from my own life, I have changed minor details to protect people's privacy.

I hope that in reading this book, you will learn how to use validation to be a positive force in people's lives.

# Part 1: Validation Basics

# What Is Validation?

Imagine you're suddenly living a nightmare. *Your* worst nightmare. Maybe you're stranded on a desert island and you'll be all alone for the rest of your life. Maybe you're trapped in a tiny closet with ten other people all day long. Maybe you have already lived a nightmare, or are living one right now. Just take a moment to think about your personal worst nightmare, whatever that might be.

Now, imagine that you live in a world where this thing is only a nightmare to *you*, and is perfectly normal and acceptable to everyone else. No one blinks an eye when you tell them about the horrible mess you're in. Everyone treats your crisis as a minor inconvenience, as a normal part of life. As months pass and your nightmare worsens, everybody looks down on you, wondering what is wrong with you and why you can't handle something that they don't see as a problem. Imagine this scenario for a moment, and think about how this makes you feel.

What you have just imagined is a reality that a lot of people experience every day. It may be a reality that you experience, and it may also be a reality that you contribute to in other people's lives. What you have just imagined is an example of invalidation.

Invalidation occurs when you do not take a person's problem seriously or when you tell them that their feelings are not legitimate. Think of a time when you had a problem, and you tried to talk to someone about it, but the other person just didn't get it. They didn't understand why the problem mattered so much to you, and they thought that you shouldn't be so upset over it. This person invalidated you.

Now, think of a time when you talked to someone about a problem, and they *did* understand. They completely accepted how you felt about the problem and how much it mattered to you, and they were willing to listen without pushing you to feel differently. In this case, the person validated you.

What is validation? When something is valid, it means that it is real. When you validate someone, you accept their feelings as legitimate. Validation means that everyone is entitled to be who they are and to feel the way they feel. It means that when a friend tells you that they feel a certain way about a particular situation, you treat their feelings as completely legitimate, even if you wouldn't feel the same way yourself. Even if most people wouldn't feel the same way. Even if you think they should feel differently. When it comes to someone's feelings, there is no "should."

Here are some basic examples of validating and invalidating responses:

Statement: "I lost my favorite shirt."
Invalidating response: "It's just a shirt."
Validating response: "I'm sorry, that sucks."

Statement: "They're all out of my favorite kind of coffee."
Invalidating response: "It's just coffee."
Validating response: "That's annoying."

Statement: "I didn't make the team."
Invalidating response: "It's just a team. Get over it."
Validating response: "That sucks. I know how important the team is to you."

The invalidating responses indicate that the issue the person is complaining about should not matter, while the validating responses acknowledge and accept how the person feels.

Think about how good it would feel if you always knew how to help your friends when something was wrong. Imagine that, even when other people put one of your friends down for being angrier, more nervous, more upset, or more excited than they "should" be, your friend knows that they can come to you and feel like their feelings are completely valid. When a friend is fuming because of a fight they had with a family member, they know you'll listen and take them seriously, so they always feel like they have someone to support them. When a friend is stressed out about the amount of work they have to do, they know you'll respond with understanding, and they never pause to worry that you might judge them just because you can do the same kind of work more easily. When a friend is upset after going through a breakup, and they just need to cry for hours or for days, they know they can get the compassion they need, and they never feel like they have to pull themself up and function before they're ready.

Most of us want to be positive forces in other people's lives. But often, the only thing we can think of is to talk people out of their

4

negative feelings, or pressure them into being happy even when something bad is happening. This book will demonstrate how to be a positive force in a different way – how to validate people in your everyday life, no matter how they feel. By validating your friends, you can form stronger relationships with them, and you can help them to feel better about who they are.

## The Most Important Conversation to Have

When we care for our pets, we understand that every pet is different. You wouldn't expect your turtle to play fetch with you. You wouldn't put your parrot on a leash and expect to walk it. You wouldn't keep your cat in a fishbowl full of water. You understand that different kinds of pets have different needs, and that in some cases, it would be downright cruel to treat one kind of pet the way you would treat another.

The same is true of people. We all have different needs, and what makes one person happy could make someone else miserable. There are lots of different ways to be supportive, and what works for one person will not work for someone else. In order to help someone, it's always important to understand what kinds of things will be most helpful to that person in particular. Try the following exercises to learn more about how you would like to be supported:

Exercise: Answer the following questions about yourself. There are no right or wrong answers. You may find that your answers are different depending on the type of situation that you are dealing with or the gravity of the issue. Pick as many choices as apply.

1. When I'm upset about something, I like a friend to support me by:

    A. Letting me talk about the upsetting thing for as long as I want to talk about it.

    B. Getting my mind off the problem with something fun.

    C. Helping me to solve the problem or improve the situation I'm in.

    D. Reminding me of all the things I still have to be happy about.

    E. Other: _____

2. If I've been upset about the same thing for a very long time, I would like my friends to:

    A. Let me feel the way that I feel and not push me to feel any differently.

    B. Push me to get back on my feet again and function the way I did before.

    C. Continue to acknowledge the problem and ask me how I'm doing every day.

    D. Keep inviting me to do fun things as if nothing is wrong, so that I can feel back to normal.

    E. Other:_____

4. When I have a problem, I normally prefer to:
>   A. Do something that is directly related to the problem, such as confronting a person about how they hurt me or working towards a change.
>   B. Vent about it to my friends, so that I can feel like someone understands.
>   C. Do something distracting to make myself feel better and forget about the problem.
>   D. Other:_____

5. When I'm feeling bad, I usually want to be:
>   A. Alone.
>   B. With one or two close friends.
>   C. With a large group of friends.
>   D. Out meeting new people.
>   E. Other:_____

6. The kind of activity that normally makes me feel better when I'm feeling bad is:
>   A. Doing something alone that is relaxing, such as taking a bubble bath or cuddling with a pet.
>   B. Doing something alone that is physically stimulating, such as walking or swimming.
>   C. Doing something alone that is mentally stimulating, such as reading a book or working on a personal project.
>   D. Talking about what is wrong with a close friend or family member.
>   E. Cuddling with a friend or family member.
>   F. Doing a low-key activity with a friend, such as playing a board game.
>   G. Doing something very stimulating with one friend, such as going dancing, going to a street fair, or visiting a place I've never been before.
>   H. Going to a big party with lots of friends.
>   I. Getting a big group together and going on a fun adventure.
>   J. Doing something physically active with lots of people, such as playing sports.
>   K. Other:_____

Now, go through each of the answer choices on all of the above questions and ask yourself how you would feel about them. Give each answer a rating between -5 and +5, with +5 being something that would make you feel much better, 0 being something that would have no effect, and -5 being something that would make you feel much worse. Again, there are no right or wrong answers. This is an exercise in self-knowledge.

Look over your answers. With the last question in particular, you may find that some activities you normally enjoy may not be so enjoyable when you're feeling bad. Compare it to when you are physically ill: Even if you normally love to go on roller coasters that flip you upside down, you probably won't want to do that while you have the flu. The same can be true when you are not feeling well emotionally. Maybe you enjoy going to big events with lots of people when you're in a good mood, but would rather do something quieter when you're upset. Or maybe you normally like to sit and talk with your friends for hours, but when something is wrong, you would rather be distracted by a big activity.

*All* of the choices in this exercise are common things that people do or recommend to make someone feel better. There are no choices that are intentionally mean or hurtful. But you will probably find that not all of these choices would help you and that some of them would actually make you feel worse. This is because everyone is different. There is no single, universal way to make someone feel better in any situation.

Just because a "helpful" quote or piece of advice is popular does not mean that it will help everyone. See how you personally feel about these common examples:

1. When I'm having a hard time and someone tells me, "What doesn't kill you makes you stronger," I feel:

    A. Better. It's comforting to know that something good will come from an otherwise bad situation.

    B. Worse. I want to just think of the bad thing as bad, and I feel like they're telling me I can't do that.

    C. Other:_____

2. If I'm worried about something and someone tells me, "Relax, everything is going to be fine," I feel:

    A. Better. I needed that reassurance.

    B. Annoyed. I feel like they didn't address my concerns. How do they know it's going to be fine?

    C. Other:_____

3. Do I believe in an afterlife? If someone close to me died, would it be a comfort for someone to tell me that they are in a better place?

    A. Yes.

    B. No.

    C. Other:_____

4. Do I believe in fate or destiny? Would I find it comforting for someone to tell me that everything happens for a reason or is meant to be?

    A. Yes.

    B. No.

    C. Other:_____

5. When someone tells me to look on the bright side of things, I feel:

    A. Better. Sometimes I get caught up in negative stuff and need a reminder of all the nice things in my life.

    B. Worse. If I am talking about something that's wrong, I don't want to be pushed to feel differently or think about other things.

    C. Other:_____

6. When someone tells me that life is 10% what happens and 90% how you react to it, I feel:

    A. Empowered. It's nice to feel more control over my own situation.

    B. Invalidated, like I'm being blamed for something that isn't my fault.

    C. Other:_____

7. How do I feel about the Eleanor Roosevelt quote, "No one can make you feel inferior without your consent?"

    A. Empowered. It makes me feel like I don't have to feel inferior just because of what someone else said.

    B. Invalidated, because when I feel inferior, I know I did not consent to it.

    C. Other:_____

Your answers may be different in different situations, or you may find yourself answering a combination of yes and no. Continue this exercise by adding other common "helpful" phrases that you have heard people say, and notice how different things make you feel:

8. Common helpful statement:_____

How it makes me feel:_____

9. Common helpful statement:_____

How it makes me feel:_____

10. Common helpful statement:_____

How it makes me feel:_____

List five things people said or did for you when you were upset that really helped you:

1._____

2._____

3._____

4._____

5._____

List five things people said or did when you were upset that made you feel worse, even if they were trying to be helpful:

1._____

2._____

3._____

4._____

5._____

The purpose of this exercise is to show how many different ways there are to support someone, and just how different our individual needs can be. We need to understand each other's individual needs, or else we'll all be pulling fish out of the water to save them from drowning.

Go through all of these exercises with the people you care about, so that you can learn about their needs, and they can learn about yours. You can use these exercises (and the others you'll find throughout this book) as a guideline for talking to your friends about how they would like to be supported.

"How do you want to be supported?" is an important conversation to have with people before anything catastrophic happens. When someone is in the middle of a crisis, it can be hard or even impossible for them to communicate what they need from you. Having these conversations ahead of time is a preventative measure, like knowing what to do in a fire. Keep in mind, of course, that sometimes it is impossible to know how you'll react to something until it happens, so understand if your friend has different needs than what they told you ahead of time.

## Your Own Needs

When we invalidate others, we don't usually do it with the intention of hurting their feelings. Sometimes we brush off people's feelings because their needs clash with our own. Maybe a friend wants to tell you a long story at a moment when you need some quiet time to yourself. Maybe a friend calls you because they need help with something, but you're not able to drop what you're doing and come running. Maybe a friend is asking you for a level of a support that you just can't provide them. In all of these cases, it's important to remember that your own needs are just as valid as anyone else's. Validating someone's feelings does not mean that you are required to give them everything that they need, or to sacrifice your own needs for theirs.

Imagine that you live in New York and your friend lives three thousand miles away in San Francisco. Your friend posts online that they are stuck somewhere and need a ride home. Obviously, you cannot give them a ride home, but you would not question the fact they *need* a ride home. It is possible for your friend to need a ride home and for you to be unable to give them one; neither fact negates the other. Yet sometimes, when you are unable to give someone all of the help that they need, you feel guilty, which can lead you to invalidate their needs. If a friend is having a crisis and needs someone to come over and stay with them, but you are just not able to do that, you might feel guilty. You might feel like you should go over and stay with your friend, even it would put a lot of strain on you. To stop yourself from feeling guilty, you might tell yourself that your friend is not really having a crisis, that they are just overreacting or being dramatic. Because if that were true – if your friend does not actually need your help – then you don't need to feel bad for not going over. But like the example of a friend needing a ride when you're too far away to give one, it is possible for your friend to *need* someone to stay with them, and for you to be unable to do that. Your friend's needs and your needs are both valid. If you can remember that your own needs are valid – that it's okay that you can't always give your friends everything that they need – then you can express understanding and compassion towards your friend during their crisis, while also maintaining your boundaries of what you are able and willing to do.

When someone is looking for more attention or support than you are able to give them, try to communicate your own needs, rather than brushing off theirs. You could say something like, "I'm really sorry that happened to you! I'm having a bad day and I don't have the energy to discuss this right now. Could I call you back tomorrow?" You can also not answer a phone call or message until you *are* up for talking, rather than engaging when you don't feel well enough. When you don't have the energy to talk to someone, place the focus on yourself and your own emotional needs, rather than saying that the other person's problems are not important enough to discuss.

Sometimes, you can have specific issues that bother you and can lead you to invalidate people's feelings. When someone is discussing an issue that upsets you, try to communicate your own needs rather than shutting them down:

Your friend: "My new kitten is soooooo adorable!"
Instead of: "Yeah, whatever."
Try: "I'm glad that you love your new kitten, but ever since my cat ran away, I've really missed her and it's hard for me to talk about this. Can we change the subject?"

Your friend: "My dad grounded me so I can't go to the party this weekend! I hate him!"
Instead of: "It's just a party! Get over it!"
Try: "I understand that you're upset, but since my dad passed away, it's really hard for me to hear people say that they hate their parents. Could you please not say that around me?"

Your Friend: "So, you're coming over to help me again this weekend, right?"
Instead of: "Why do you ask me to do so much for you? Can't you do anything for yourself?"
Try: "I won't be able to do that this weekend."

Your Friend: "Let me tell you all about my surgery!"
Instead of: "Gross! Who wants to hear about that?"
Try: "I'm really sorry you had to go through surgery, and I'm so glad that it went well. I would rather not hear all the graphic details. I wish I could listen, but it's going to be too stressful for me. I'm still here for you if you want to talk about anything else, just not the graphic stuff."

If your friends continue to be insensitive to your needs once you have expressed them, it is fine to assert your boundaries. Make sure your friend understands that you value their feelings as well as your own.

Exercise: Think of a time when you brushed off someone's feelings because you just weren't up for listening at that moment, or because you were not able to do what they were asking of you. How could you have expressed your own needs and boundaries to the person without criticizing theirs?

_____

_____

_____

# The First Rule of Validation

The most basic rule of validation is that people and their feelings are fixed factors. A fixed factor is something that cannot be changed. For example, if you plan to do an outdoor activity on a particular day and it ends up raining, the rain itself is not something that can be changed. There are a number of ways to solve the problem, such as rescheduling the event to another day or doing an indoor activity instead, but you would never just go outside and tell the sky to stop raining. Validating a person means treating who they are and how they feel the same way that you would treat the rain – as something that you cannot change. This does not mean that people cannot change, but unless someone has told you that they *want* to change, it is not up to you to push change on them.

(Note: Treating someone's feelings as fixed factors does not mean that you need to treat their *behavior* as a fixed factor. If a person is doing something that is hurting you or others, you have every right to tell them to stop.)

Let's go through a few examples of how to treat a person's internal state the same way that you would treat the weather. If someone tells you, "I'm really lonely," there are a number of solutions to this problem, from making new friends where they are to packing up and moving closer to the people they know and love. What will work best for this person depends on their personality, their values, and their situation. But what is *not* okay is to indicate that they just "shouldn't" feel lonely, that they "should" be okay with the situation they are in, or that they "should" be the kind of person who doesn't get lonely or who can deal with being lonely and still be okay. You can listen, be supportive, and help them solve this problem, but you cannot simply tell them to not be that way, any more than you would tell the sky to stop raining.

Here is a more detailed example: A friend tells you, "I had no fun at that party last night! I had no one to talk to and nothing to do. I just sat there by myself the whole time." There are several reasons that this might have happened. First, it's possible that your friend would have really *liked* to socialize and participate more in the party, but their shyness got in the way. If they are telling you that they would like to be more outgoing and more able to participate in things, it might be appropriate to offer them suggestions of how to introduce themselves to

15

people or ask if they can join in. If your friend feels insecure, you could give them reassurance that they are a great person and that if someone doesn't include them when they try to be nice, it's the other person's problem and not your friend's. What is *not* okay is telling them that they need to just get over their shyness and get out there and participate. Your friend might be dealing with a level of anxiety that you have never experienced before, and it is hurtful to tell them to just get over it. Being supportive of their feelings and offering specific suggestions on how they can get better at socializing is great, but telling them that they just shouldn't be the way they are is invalidating.

Alternatively, your friend may not have been shy. It could be that your friend tried to engage with other people, but the other people were not very welcoming and made them feel left out. This is a problem with the people at the party, *not* with your friend. Not everyone wants to keep pushing and fighting their way into a group when the group isn't very welcoming. That's not a very fun way to spend a party. Don't place the blame on your friend for something that others did to them. Reassure them that it's not their fault, and see if you can find other parties that are more welcoming.

Finally, your friend may have just not *wanted* to participate in the available activities at the party. Maybe your friend just doesn't like large parties with lots of people they don't know. (This is different from being shy but still *wanting* to talk to new people). Maybe your friend prefers smaller gatherings. Maybe your friend thought that more people they knew would be at the party. Maybe your friend assumed they'd get to stick by their friends all night, but their friends dispersed without them. Maybe everyone was doing activities that your friend doesn't like. Your friend may have made a mistake and not known what the party would be like. Your friend may have been pressured into going to the party when they knew they wouldn't have fun. In any case, the important thing is that you respect your friend's right to be the way they are and *do not* try to change them. Your friend is a solid, fixed factor, and it is the party that did not suit them, not your friend that didn't suit the party. That is okay. Everyone doesn't have to like everything. Validating your friend means not trying to change them into the kind of person who would have enjoyed this party. And finally, to truly be a validating friend, you can remember what you learned about your friend from this conversation, and take that into account when you decide what events to invite them to in the future.

## Accepting People as They Are

Every time we use words to describe another person, we have the potential to be either validating or invalidating. Some ways of describing people can validate and accept who they are, but others implicitly pressure them to be something different.

I once took two personality tests. The first was the Big Five Personality Test, which measures five different personality traits, and tells you how much of each trait you have. I felt bad about myself after taking this test. It was clear to me how a person was "supposed" to come out, and I had failed the test miserably. Then, I took the Myers-Briggs Type Indicator, which measures you on four different spectrums, with sixteen possible types. I gave a lot of the same answers that I did on the Big Five test, but this time, I felt good about myself. My personality type described me perfectly, the results gave me tips on which careers were good matches for me, and most importantly, my type was just as good as the other fifteen.

So why did one test make me feel good about myself when the other test made me feel bad? The answer lies in the way that the results were presented. The Big Five test measures traits in quantities, so that getting a low score on a positive characteristic makes you feel like something is lacking. But the Myers-Briggs test treats each quality as a spectrum of two equally desirable traits. Your results do not show that you are lacking any particular trait, only that you have more of the opposite trait. For example, the Big Five test measures how extroverted you are on a scale from 0 to 100. Since our society treats extroversion as a desirable quality, getting a low score, such as 30 points out of 100, can make you feel like you failed. However, the Myers-Briggs test treats introversion and extroversion as a spectrum where everyone falls somewhere between extremely introverted and extremely extroverted. On the Myers-Briggs test, you would not be told that you scored 30 points out of 100 for extroversion – you would be told that you are 70% introverted and 30% extroverted. No matter where you are on the scale, you still have 100%. The Myers-Briggs test treats introversion and extroversion as equally desirable traits, unlike the Big Five test, which makes introverts feel like they are *lacking* one trait rather than *having* a different trait.

Whenever we think of people as either having a desirable trait or not having it, it can be easy to think that something is wrong with a

18

person who doesn't have the trait. And when you think of it that way, you may end up pushing someone to change. If someone hasn't told you that they want to change, it's not your place to push them. So, if you find yourself thinking of someone as, for instance, not outgoing, not adventurous, not flexible, etc., try to think of the person's qualities as being on a spectrum of opposite traits. See if you can come up with a positive or neutral word for the opposite of whatever trait you think the person is lacking. Picture a color spectrum of green slowing changing to blue (or whichever colors you like), where green is the "desirable" quality, and blue is the positive or neutral opposite trait that your friend has. Picture where the person probably falls on this spectrum, and remind yourself that green is not better than blue, it is just a different color. This person is not lacking green, they simply have more blue.

When you are describing someone's personality, try to describe them either in a positive way, or in a matter-of-fact a way. Avoid using words like "too." Instead of saying, "Tom is too sensitive," just say, "Tom is sensitive." The word "too" implies that there is something wrong with Tom being sensitive, whereas the second sentence just states a fact. Tom might be more sensitive than most people, but that is not a problem unless Tom says that it is a problem. The only time it is appropriate to say "too sensitive" would be if you were discussing whether or not Tom should participate in an activity that is geared towards non-sensitive people, in which case Tom could be too sensitive to participate in the activity without becoming overwhelmed. (Although in this case, you should ask Tom if he would like to participate, rather than just assuming he wouldn't). When we say something like, "It's too cold!" what we really mean is, "It's too cold for me to feel comfortable." "Too" is a relative word. When you say that something is "too much" of a certain quality, it has to be "too much" in relation to something else.

Validation means never telling someone to "suck it up," "tough it out," "get over it," "grow up," or any other phrase that pushes people to accept things that they are not okay with. Validation means eliminating words from your vocabulary that put people down specifically for having strong emotional reactions: "baby," "crybaby," "drama queen," etc. Validation also means eliminating the concept of "overreacting." It is up to each individual person to decide how much something matters to them, how strongly it makes them feel, and how they will react. The term "overreacting" implies that there is a standard

19

way that a person should react in a given situation, and that more extreme reactions are less legitimate. People react based on how much something matters to them personally. There is no such thing as "overreacting."

An important aspect of accepting people is recognizing that some things just do not mix well together. Every person is not suited for every type of activity, job, or environment, and that does not mean that anything is wrong with the person. If you uproot a palm tree from the Caribbean and stick it at the North Pole, it's not going to survive, but that does not mean that it's a bad tree.

You can become more validating by changing the language that you use when you talk about people and situations that just don't fit. For instance, when you say that someone is not college material, management material, or relationship material, you are implying that people need to measure up to a certain set of standards. Instead of saying that someone is not a certain kind of "material," try saying:
"I'm not sure if college would be a good experience for Vijay."
"I don't think a management position would be a good fit for Jordan."
"Sonia and I are not relationship-compatible."
All of these statements make it clear that nothing is wrong with the person; it is the external situation that does not fit them.

Watch out for telling people that they need to "work on" or change things that they have not expressed interest in changing. Here are some examples of how to make your language more accepting:
Instead of: "Lily needs to be more social."
Try: "Lily isn't into large social gatherings."
Instead of: "Carlos needs to break out of his comfort zone."
Try: "Carlos didn't seem interested in bungee jumping when I asked."
Instead of: "Tasha needs to be more flexible."
Try: "Tasha won't like it if we change plans on her at the last minute."

In order to sound more accepting, try to keep your tone matter-of-fact. You could say, "Tasha won't like it if we change plans" in the same tone that you would say, "It looks like it's going to rain." By speaking matter-of-factly, you are not only validating the person you are speaking about, but you are also promoting acceptance among the people you are talking to. You are showing everyone that there is nothing wrong with Tasha's personality, making them less likely to criticize Tasha and more likely to be open and accepting of people's differences in other situations. It's a win for everyone.

Exercise: Think of three instances when you said that someone needed to change something about themself that they did not tell you that they wanted to change, and practice stating the same facts with more accepting language:

1.    A. What you said:_____
       B. More accepting way of saying it:_____
2.    A. What you said:_____
       B. More accepting way of saying it:_____
3.    A. What you said:_____
       B. More accepting way of saying it:_____

## Validating People's Feelings

When a friend is telling you about a problem, pay attention to both the objective situation of what is going on and the subjective situation of how your friend feels about it. Both parts of the situation are equally important. Listening to the objective situation may help you discover solutions to the problem that your friend cannot see while they are right in the middle of it. But if you *only* listen to the objective information, you are missing part of the equation: you don't know how your friend feels about the issue or how important it is to them. If you only pay attention to the objective situation, you may only think about how *you* would react to the same situation. You might think, "That situation doesn't sound as bad as my friend is making it out to be." Pay attention not only to *what* your friend says, but also to the *way* that they say it. Does your friend refer to their situation as "horrible" or just "annoying?" Does their tone indicate that this is a major problem, or a minor one? How upset/angry/scared do they seem to be because of this problem? *That* tells you how bad the problem is, not the situation itself.

One major context clue is the circumstance under which someone is telling you about the problem. If someone called, emailed, or asked to meet up with you specifically to talk about this problem, that means that it is important. This is not to say that a problem is automatically less important if it comes up in conversation when you're already together, but if someone especially contacted you because of the problem, you can assume that it matters a lot to them. Once you have an idea of how important the issue is for your friend, keep that importance level in mind. Don't start thinking about how you or other people would react differently to the same problem.

Listen to your friend for as long as they need to talk, without interrupting. Pay close attention to what they are saying – both the facts of the situation and how they feel. If you think of advice or comments while your friend is talking, hold onto them until later. Focus your attention on just listening to your friend.

After your friend has finished talking, briefly repeat their own story back to them to make sure that you understand. This will let them know that you listened and will allow them to clarify anything that you misunderstood. Ask them questions. As you discuss the issue with your friend, keep paying attention to how much importance they are giving it, and make sure your tone and choice of words show that you are taking the problem as seriously as they have indicated it is. Repeat what they've said and affirm that you are taking it seriously. For instance, if someone called your friend a rude name, you could say, "He really said that to you? That is so disrespectful!" Obviously your friend already knows that this person said something disrespectful to them, but this simple statement shows that you listened and you care about their problem.

When discussing a problem that is happening to your friend, be careful not to put the blame on them for having the problem. For example: A friend tells you that they can't get any sleep because their dorm is too loud at night. If you say something like, "It's really so loud that you can't sleep?" that could mean two different things – it could be criticizing the dorm for being too loud, or it could be criticizing your friend for being too light of a sleeper. Or often, a combination of the two. There is nothing wrong with the statement itself, but you should make sure that you really are criticizing the dorm situation and not your friend. Now, if you're comfortable living with a similar amount of noise, you might be surprised that it is a problem for someone else. It's perfectly okay if a problem is unfamiliar to you. The way to handle this is to remember that your friend's feelings are fixed factors that are not up for debate. Once you accept that your friend's inability to sleep with noise is not negotiable, it becomes easier to treat the noise itself as the problem. Try saying, "It's really so loud that you can't sleep? That sucks!" Adding "That sucks!" on the end affirms that you are taking your friend's problem seriously and are not putting the blame on them. After some affirmation, you can ask your friend about possible solutions, such as moving to a quieter dorm.

When you're on the outside of a situation, it is sometimes easy to find solutions that a person in the middle of the conflict cannot see. The advice you have to offer could be valuable and completely turn your friend's situation around. Just be sure that you always validate the problem itself *before* offering a solution. Look at these two examples:
Example 1:
Friend: "I haven't slept for a week because the new streetlight shines right into my window."
You: "Why don't you just get a curtain?"

Example 2:
Friend: "I haven't slept for a week because the new streetlight shines right into my window."
You: "You haven't gotten any sleep all week? Wow, that sounds miserable! Have you thought about using a curtain to block the light? Or if you don't want to pay for a new curtain, draping a blanket over the curtain rod might work."

Notice the differences between these two responses. While you offer the same advice in each situation, you do several things in the second example that you do not in the first:

1. You validated your friend's feelings before offering advice. Your friend already had a miserable week of no sleep, so it's good to offer sympathy for that, even if you also solve the problem going forward. Validating also lets your friend know that you are taking their problem seriously, whereas the tone in Example 1 might say, "There's an easy solution, so what's the problem?"

2. You respected the fact that your friend may not have thought of a solution while the problem was happening to them, even though the solution seems obvious to an outsider. The tone in Example 1 could sound like a put-down, indicating that your friend should have figured out the solution on their own.

3. In Example 2, you *offer* the advice as a suggestion, rather than stating it as the only solution. You also acknowledge that getting heavy curtains may not work for your friend, since curtains cost money. It's also possible that your friend has a different reason that curtains wouldn't work, one that you haven't considered. Be open to feedback if your suggestion doesn't work for them, and show that you are willing to consider alternatives, rather than pushing one specific solution on them.

When your friend has good news to share with you, it is equally important to respond with validation. Sometimes your friends will be extremely excited about things that are not a big deal to you. Maybe your friend is psyched about making the swim team, while you're a much better swimmer than they are and don't see making the team as an accomplishment. When this is the case, use the tips we discussed in this chapter to validate your friend's feelings of excitement. Pay attention to your friend's *subjective* experience – how excited and proud they feel – and react based on their feelings, rather than what you think about the accomplishment itself. Even if you're the best swimmer in your district, even if you made the team when you were five years old, even if you're training for the Olympics and think your hometown swim team is a joke – congratulate your friend, celebrate with them, and let them feel good about themself.

# Understanding the Problem

When a friend is talking to you about a problem, it is important to understand *what* the issue is, before you comment or offer advice. Imagine that your friend got a new haircut, other people are making fun of it, and your friend is upset. It's possible that your friend is upset because they hate their new haircut. It's also possible that your friend loves their new haircut and is upset because people are laughing at them. If you say something like, "Don't worry, your hair will grow back," you might hurt your friend's feelings if they like their new haircut. Alternatively, if you say something like, "Your haircut looks fine!" your friend might feel invalidated if they hate their haircut. It's better to first ask your friend how they feel about their own haircut so that you can offer them the kind of validation that they need.

Or imagine that your friend used to be an avid blogger, but they tell you that they haven't had time to blog lately because they've been so busy with their job. It's possible that your friend *wants* to focus their job at the moment, and having less time to blog is not a problem to them. It's also possible that your friend wants to be blogging more, and they are upset that they don't have time for it. If you say something like, "That's okay, life happens," when your friend is angry that they don't have time to blog, you would be invalidating their feelings and not respecting their priorities. But if you automatically start advising your friend on how to cram blogging into their tight schedule, they may feel pressured to work it in when they would actually prefer to take a break. In order to validate your friend, remember to ask them how they feel so that you understand exactly what the problem is.

## Tip of the Iceberg

One of the most important steps to validating someone is simply listening. Listen all the way through, to everything that someone has to say, without cutting them off. You may have helpful advice, but store that in your back pocket for the time being and just let your friend get out everything that they need to say. This alone will make your friend feel heard and validated.

Sometimes, a problem that someone is talking about is just the tip of the iceberg, meaning that the initial issue they are complaining about is part of a much bigger, deeper issue that you are not aware of, and possibly, that they are not even aware of. Here is an example:

Scenario 1:

Friend: "My stepmom bought me the ugliest quilt in the world! It's pea-green and covered with orange grasshoppers! Grasshoppers aren't even orange and who the heck wants bugs on their bed? It's the ugliest quilt I ever-"

You: "Why don't you just flip the quilt over and use the plain side?"

Friend: "Um, yeah, I guess..."

Now, there is nothing wrong with your suggestion. You did validate the problem by offering a clever solution, rather than saying, "It's just a quilt!" But by cutting your friend off, she does not get the chance to finish expressing her feelings, and you may not be getting the full story of what is wrong.

Scenario 2:

Friend: "My stepmom bought me the ugliest quilt in the world! It's pea-green and covered with orange grasshoppers! Grasshoppers aren't even orange and who the heck wants bugs on their bed? It's the ugliest quilt I ever saw! Why does she have to ruin everything? What's wrong with my old quilt that my mom made for me? My mom just died last year and now my stepmom is ruining our whole house with all her stuff and my dad's acting like my mom was never even here!"

In this case, what your friend said about her new quilt was only the tip of the iceberg, the surface of a much deeper problem that can't be fixed just by flipping the quilt over.

Sometimes when someone is in the midst of a crisis, they may complain about smaller things first, only to realize that those things are part of a much larger issue. When you're in a crisis, that can make everything feel bad, even things that wouldn't normally bother you. In the example above, your friend may not have cared about the quilt at all if the circumstance were different. When you cut her off early, you stopped her from reaching the root of the problem. But when you listened to your friend, you allowed her to get to the heart of the matter and share what was really bothering her.

A conflict that seems minor to you will not *always* be the tip of the iceberg. Sometimes people will simply care more about certain things than you do. But it's good to keep in mind that something can be just the surface of a much deeper problem, and the best way to help someone uncover that problem is to listen.

## Get the Whole Story

It's easy to think that someone is "overreacting" to something when you only see a tiny piece of what is going on. But keep in mind that everyone is coming from a different place, and you may not be getting the full story. Imagine the following scenario:

Matt and Jason are meeting each other for lunch in a mall food court. Matt asks Jason, "Wanna go get a hamburger?"

Jason exclaims, "Are you kidding me??!!" and storms out without another word to Matt.

Now, at first glance, you may not understand why Jason reacted this way. It may look as if he got upset over nothing. But now imagine this backstory:

Jason has been a vegetarian for five years, and Matt has never accepted it. Matt has constantly criticized Jason for his decision, made fun of him in front of their other friends, and pressured him to eat meat. Jason has told Matt many times to cut it out, and Matt usually leaves him alone for a while, but eventually, he always starts harassing Jason again. Jason recently had another discussion with Matt about accepting his decision, and in that discussion, Matt promised to be more considerate. When Matt asked Jason to get a hamburger soon after that discussion, it was the last straw.

With this new information, Jason's reaction doesn't seem so strange anymore. It can be easy to think that someone is upset over "nothing" when you don't have all of the information. When you don't understand someone's actions, it helps to ask them what's going on and listen to the full story.

## Is This Good or Bad?

Sometimes it's easy to tell how a friend feels about something, but other times, you might not be so sure. Sometimes people communicate in a different way than you do, and sometimes people don't express their feelings outwardly at all. A great way to be validating is to ask your friend how they feel about something, rather than guessing at how they feel. If your friend tells you something, and you are unsure whether they are sharing good news or bad news, just ask, "Is that good or bad?" If you guess, you might guess wrong. And even though you'd hope that your friend would simply correct you, that may not always happen. If you assume that something is good news when it is actually bad news, even if it was an honest mistake on your part, your friend may not have the courage to tell you the truth, especially if it's something that most people would be happy about. Consider this scenario:

[Content: emotional abuse] For Aaron's birthday this year, his mom surprises him with something extra-special – a trip to visit her in New York City for a whole week! While lots of people would jump at this opportunity, Aaron is devastated. He lives with his dad most of the year and always dreads getting together with his mom. Aaron's mom acts like she misses him and wishes he would visit more, whenever he arrives for a visit, within a few hours, Aaron's mom always ends up calling him names, putting him down for almost everything he does, and making him feel worthless. Aaron feels like he can never do anything right in her eyes, and he always leaves their visits feeling miserable for weeks. Aaron tries to come up with excuses for why he can't spend the week with her, but his dad keeps saying, "You'll have a great time!"

When Aaron meets his friend Naomi at lunch, he tells her, "My mom invited me to spend a week with her in New York." Naomi is not able to read how Aaron feels about this trip from his tone or facial expression, so she makes her own assumptions: "That's great, Aaron! My parents are divorced too and I *never* get to see my dad! I'm lucky if he calls once a year. You are so lucky to get to spend the whole winter break with your mom!"

Aaron wants to tell Naomi the truth, but now that Naomi has assumed the news was good, Aaron feels guilty admitting that he doesn't want to go. He knows that it's a privilege to be able to spend that week with his mom, and that a lot of his peers, like Naomi, wish that they had the same opportunity. Aaron is afraid that Naomi will judge him for being ungrateful if he admits that he doesn't want to go, so he goes along with her response and says, "Yeah, I guess it will be nice to spend the time with my mom."

Because Aaron couldn't tell Naomi how he really feels, things might go a lot worse for him. Aaron's dad thinks that the trip will be great for him, and Aaron has not yet found the courage to tell his dad why he does not want to go. He is scared that his dad might not believe him or might think that he is exaggerating about how deeply his mom's behavior affects him. Discussing this issue with a friend could have been a great opportunity for him to work through his feelings about visiting his mom, in a context where he wouldn't have to feel guilty or pressured. If Aaron had been able to discuss the situation with Naomi, Naomi could have validated Aaron's feelings. Then the two of them might have figured out that Aaron needed to talk to his dad about not visiting his mom, and they could have worked through what he should say. But because they lost the opportunity to have this conversation, Aaron may not have the conversation with his dad at all. When Naomi assumed that Aaron would be happy rather than asking how he felt, that was seemingly a small difference, but it could make the difference as to whether Aaron continues to visit his mom and feel miserable, or whether he finds the courage to talk to his dad about what is going on.

When you're already worried that people won't take you seriously or respect your feelings, especially when you have negative feelings about something that most people would be happy about, it can be very difficult to correct someone and say, "No, this is actually bad news." So, if you are helping a friend and you are unsure whether something is good or bad, don't make a guess – just ask your friend, "Is that good or bad news?" or "How are you feeling about that?" and be open to whatever response they give.

## When You Just Don't Get It

We've talked about what to do when your friend is upset about something that makes you think, "What's the big deal?" But what do you do when you truly do not understand what the problem is at all? You wouldn't want to end up doing something like this:

Sean: "You won't believe what happened this morning – I was backing out of the driveway and I hit my neighbor's car!"

Ashley: "So? What's the problem?"

We can probably all agree that "So what?" is an insensitive response in this situation. But the *reason* Ashley sounds so uncaring is that we can all agree that hitting a neighbor's car is bad. It's hard to imagine that Ashley could honestly not understand why Sean is upset.

But what happens when someone has a problem that is not so obvious? What if someone sounds as distressed as Sean sounds in the example above, but you honestly do not understand what the problem is? If you ask, "What's the problem?" the way that Ashley does above, you will sound like you don't care, because to them, the problem could be just as obviously bad as hitting the neighbor's car.

Whatever you do, do not say, "So what?" or "What's wrong with that?" when someone has reached the end of telling you about a problem. This kind of subtle invalidation could make the person second-guess themself. They could internalize the idea that they *should* be okay with whatever is going on and be too scared to reach out for help.

It is good to ask your friend questions if you do not understand, but make sure that your tone implies that you do accept the problem, and that you do not have a tone of "That's all?"

Here is an example: A friend tells you, "My dorm is very social! Everyone leaves their bedroom doors open and people are always talking and hanging out together!" Your friend sounds upset. Their tone indicates that this is a problem, but to you, what they said sounds perfectly fine. Dorms are supposed to be social! You don't see what the issue is. How do you find out?

Before saying anything to your friend, tell yourself, *This is a problem for my friend. I don't know why it is a problem at this point, but I do know that it is a problem.* Just take a moment to remind yourself of that before saying anything. Next, repeat what your friend just said back to them, in about the same tone that they said it to you: "So everyone in your dorm is really social and leaves their doors open?" Your friend will probably respond with something like, "Yeah, my roommates always leave the door open and people walk into my room without even asking! I have no privacy or alone time here!" By repeating what your friend said as a question, you are prompting them to provide more information about the situation. This is probably the easiest way to find out what's wrong. Also, saying something like, "And you don't like that, right?" affirms that the situation is a problem, and might prompt your friend to share more information. If this technique does not work, you can ask your friend directly what is wrong, but try to ask in an understanding tone. You could say something like, "Sorry, but I'm actually having trouble understanding which part of this is hurting you. Can you help me understand?"

If you are ever unsure of how your friend feels about something – if you can't tell from their tone whether, "My dorm is really social!"

is positive or negative – it never hurts to ask your friend how they feel about it.

Keep in mind that you won't always get it. You may never quite understand why something is a problem to someone else, and they may not be able to explain it in a way that you can understand. That's okay. Just try your best to be supportive and validating anyway, and keep in mind that if something is a problem for someone else, it *is* a problem even if you never fully understand the issue. Remember that to them, the problem might be obvious, the same way that is was obvious why Sean was upset about hitting the neighbor's car.

# Digital Communication

Most of the advice in this book applies just as well when you are typing instead of talking. But watching your words becomes more important when the other person can't hear your tone or see your body language. In the example of saying, "It's really so loud that you can't sleep? That sucks!" in response to a friend living in a noisy dorm, the "That sucks!" part becomes even more important when you are typing. Without those words, your friend probably won't be able to tell that you are criticizing the dorm and not their sensitivity to the noise. If your friend has already sought help and not been taken seriously, they could interpret your reaction as not taking them seriously. When typing, it is good to follow questions like this one with statements like, "That sucks," "That wasn't nice of that person," etc., so your friend knows that you are reacting to how bad the problem is, not questioning whether it is actually that bad.

Pay attention to the words, punctuation, and emoji that your friend uses and try to match them. For instance, if your friend writes, "THIS SUCKS!!!!" don't write back, "That's annoying," or "That's inconvenient." Using less intense words is a subtle form of invalidation. If someone refers to something as "horrible" and then you refer their problem as an "inconvenience," you are taking the problem down to lesser importance than what they are communicating. Try to match their words as best you can.

It is also helpful to match your friend on other aspects of their message, such as using the same punctuation and capitalization that they are using. If your friend posts a message such as:

"My boyfriend's been CHEATING on me for 2 MONTHS!!!!!! I just found out and he's claiming it's my fault but it's NOT my fault HE'S THE ONE WHO CHEATED!!!!!!! >:-( "

Try typing a response like:

"I am so sorry!!! That was NOT okay at all!!!"

"It is absolutely NOT your fault!"

If you don't feel as angry as your friend does and don't feel right matching their exact tone, try something like:

"I am so sorry. That was a horrible thing for him to do. It is not your fault at all!"

"I'm so sorry! *lots of hugs* <3 <3 <3"

"I'm sorry :-( I'm here if you want to talk. <3"

While these responses do not match your friend's tone precisely, they still keep the magnitude of situation the same by using words like "horrible," assuring your friend that it is not their fault, offering virtual hugs when you can't give them real hugs right away, and offering to listen.

Another thing to keep in mind when you're typing is not to put other people's statements in quotations. Check out these examples:

A. You found the joke offensive.

B. You found the joke "offensive."

A. You said that your friends disowned you.

B. You said that your friends "disowned" you.

A. You said you have too much going on.

B. You said you have "too much" going on.

All of the sentences labeled "A" simply state facts, but the sentences labeled "B" say, "You *claim* that this happened, but it is actually not true." The quotations automatically invalidate the words inside them. If someone found a joke to be offensive, then it was offensive to them. Putting the word "offensive" in quotes is the same as saying, "That was not offensive – you're overreacting." Avoid critiquing people's choice of words when they describe their feelings – if someone says, "My friends totally disowned me!" you know what they mean, even if you normally only use the concept of "disowning" with family members. There is no reason to correct their word choice.

It's always good to ask people how they are feeling, rather than assuming. But when you need to make a guess about how important someone's problem is, it is better to guess higher rather than lower. It is much easier for a friend to say, "Actually, it's not that bad. I'm okay," than it is to say, "Actually, I'm not okay." Imagine that you missed a day of work yesterday because you were very sick. Today, you're back, but you still feel under the weather. Your boss assumes that you are fine again and expects you to function at full force. What would you do? You might not feel comfortable saying how bad you feel, and you may push yourself to function normally because your boss expects it. Now, imagine that you missed work yesterday because you were sick, but today you're in tip-top shape again. But this time, your boss assumes that you're not feeling well and encourages you to take it slow. How would you react in this case? Chances are, this wouldn't bother you; if you wanted to tell your boss that you were feeling better, you wouldn't feel pressured to hide it. When in doubt, it is better to treat someone's problem more seriously, rather than less seriously. It is much easier to tell someone that you are actually okay when they are concerned than it is to tell someone that you are actually *not* okay when they assume you are fine.

Finally, keep in mind that validating people on the Internet is just as important as validating people in real life. This does not mean that you need to leave a validating comment on every single post or thread that you read, but it does mean that leaving an *invalidating* comment on a thread – for instance, commenting that someone's problem isn't real and that they need to get over themself – is just as bad online as it is in real life. When you respond to online threads, remember that the original poster is in fact a real person who is probably looking for support. One of the great things about the Internet is that we can meet people who are going through similar issues, and we have an opportunity to support each other. If a thread starts with a post about a problem, it's especially important to keep it clear of invalidating comments, because they not only invalidate the original poster, but also the other readers who can relate to the original post and came to the page for support. And what's more, invalidating comments can scare those readers into not sharing their feelings and seeking the support that they need, for fear that other people will respond the same way.

## Giving Control

A lot of difficult things that people go through are things outside of their control – the death of a loved one, parents getting divorced, being harassed or assaulted, etc. The best thing that you can give someone is control over their own life. One part of validating someone is letting them make their own choices and respecting their choices, even if they are not doing what you would have done. If a friend tells you that somebody hurt them, don't immediately start telling them what they "need" to do about it. Although your intentions are good, your friend has already had their boundaries violated. You want to put your friend back in control of their own life by listening and *asking* them what they want to do about the problem. Try asking questions like, "How do you want to handle this problem?" and "What will make you feel better?" Let your friend know that you will support them no matter what they choose.

Keep in mind, also, that you do not know someone's situation as well as they do. Before you go and confront someone on your friend's behalf, *ask* your friend if they would like you to do that. While it's great that you want to stand up for your friend, your friend might know that the person will treat them even worse if you confront them in that way. If your friend says that they don't want to talk to their parents about something, don't push them to talk to their parents. Your friend may not have the same relationship with their parents that you have with yours, and they might know that the talk would be ineffective or would make the situation worse. If someone is ever in immediate danger, you need to step in to help them, but when it comes to issues that are not immediately dangerous, be supportive in a way that lets your friend have control.

## Using Validation with Reassurance

When someone is worried about the outcome of a situation, validating their worry is not always enough. Often, they will need reassurance, in addition to validation.

What is the difference between validation and reassurance? Validation means acknowledging and accepting the person's worry as a perfectly legitimate way to feel, while reassurance involves easing their fears by letting them know that things should be okay. Sometimes a person needs more validation, and other times they need more reassurance. Here is an example of the difference:

Validating response: "It's okay to be upset that your mom is getting remarried. This is going to be a big change for your family."

Reassuring response: "You'll be okay. Everything is going to be fine."

Both of these responses are good, but they would be even better combined. Validating the person's feelings is great, but validation alone, with no reassurance, may not help the person to feel better. Depending on your tone, it could even make the person feel like being upset is inevitable and they cannot do anything to feel better about their mom's remarriage. Reassurance without validation – even though you intend to ease the person's concerns – can make the person feel like you are brushing aside their feelings. Reassuring someone with a general statement like, "Everything is going to be fine," does not show that you understand their feelings. The best response would be to find a way to combine validation and reassurance together. Here is one way to combine the two:

1.      Validate the person's feelings first. Start by saying something like, "Having your mom get remarried can be difficult," "It's okay that you're having a hard time with this," "I had a hard time when my dad remarried as well."

2.      Listen to what the person is upset about. Are they worried that their relationship with their mom will not be the same anymore? Do they feel like they would be betraying their dad by having a relationship with their stepdad? Are they scared about moving to a new place, or having new people move into their home? Do they just not like their new stepfamily? Let your friend talk about their concerns. Then, discuss some strategies for dealing with each of their problems. If you *are* the parent, you can reassure your child that their relationship with you will not change and that they are not betraying anyone by liking their new

stepparent. Just saying, "Everything will be fine," is not always effective, but letting them know *how* everything will be fine could make them feel much better.

3.      Sometimes, a person just needs more reassurance than validation. If someone is afraid that they'll never have the same relationship with their mom again, just saying, "Yeah, that's hard," could reinforce the idea that this is true and there is nothing that they can do about it. In a case like this, they need reassurance. This would be a time to assure them that their mom is their mom and that relationship will not change.

## Respecting Boundaries

Imagine that you stopped by your friend's home so that they could grab something, but they are reluctant to let you inside:

Friend: "I don't want you to see messy my apartment is!"

You: "I don't care what your apartment looks like."

Friend: "No, really, I don't want you to see it."

You: "It's no big deal – my house is a mess too! I'm not going to judge, I promise."

It's great to let your friend know that they are safe with you and that you're not going to judge them for having a messy apartment. That is a sign that you are a good friend. But remember that as much as you'd like to, you cannot just make your friend feel comfortable with something they are not comfortable with. You may not see the issue, but your friend might feel very self-conscious about the inside of their apartment, especially if their home isn't as nice as yours. It's good to let your friend know that you don't care how their home looks, but you should also respect the fact that they might still want to keep it private. Here is a better alternative:

Friend: "I don't want you to see messy my apartment is!"

You: "I don't care what your apartment looks like."

Friend: "No, really, I don't want you to see it."

You: "Okay, I can wait outside while your grab your coat. But if you ever do want to show me your apartment, I promise I won't judge how it looks."

[Content: body image] Here is another example:

Friend: "I don't want to wear my bathing suit at the party! I hate the way I look!"

You: "What are you talking about? You look great in a bathing suit!"

Friend: "I'm really not comfortable. I need to lose weight."

You: "You do not need to lose weight! You look beautiful just the way you are."

Friend: "I don't know…"

You: "Come on! Everyone's gonna think you look cute in your bathing suit!"

Friend: "I guess…"

Now, it's wonderful that you want to help your friend feel better about their body. That in itself is a positive response. But keep in mind that body image is a complex issue, and as much as you want to, you

39

cannot just make your friend feel comfortable with their body when they don't. A better approach would be to let your friend know that they look fine, but also accept their choice to do what they want with their body, which may or may not involve wearing a bathing suit:

Friend: "I don't want to wear my bathing suit at the party. I hate the way I look!"

You: "If you'd rather not wear a bathing suit, that's totally fine. But I do think you look great just the way you are!"

Or:

You: "Your body is fine just the way it is and you are entitled to wear what you want regardless of how you look. But if you'd rather not, that's also perfectly okay."

# Asking Questions

When you ask someone a question, you are inviting them to share their thoughts and feelings with you, so it is important for you to be respectful of their answer. The same way that you would make sure guests feel comfortable when you invite them into your home, you should be providing a safe space for someone when you invite them to share their thoughts and feelings with you.

If you ask someone to share their favorite book, band, movie, or TV show, be open to whatever they might answer, even if you think their favorite movie is for five-year-olds or that your dog can sing better than their favorite band. It's perfectly fine say that you're not really into your friend's favorite band, but you shouldn't put them down for their response. In group settings where you are sharing your favorites as an ice-breaker activity, make it clear that all answers are welcome. If you are leading the group, make sure that the group is respectful enough to handle anybody's answers to the questions, and be prepared to stand up for anyone if people make fun of their answer.

When you ask questions with the expectation that a person will give you a particular response, you can subtly invalidate their feelings and make it harder for them to tell you the truth. For example, asking, "How was school today?" in a neutral tone is more validating than asking, "Did you have fun at school today?" in an upbeat tone, which might imply that you expect the answer to be "yes."

In my first year of college, we had a start-of-the-year orientation camping trip that almost everyone loved. I had a miserable time on the trip. I hated camping and did not bond with any of the people in my group. When we got back to campus, everyone was going on about how much fun they had had on their trips. When my classmates saw that I was not as enthusiastic as they were, several of them asked me, "Did you not like your trip???!!!" The way they asked it, you wouldn't write it with just one question mark. You'd write it with several exclamation points, because they were so shocked at the idea that I could have had a different experience than they did. While it was technically a question, the way they asked me implied that I should have loved my trip and that there was something wrong with me if I didn't.

Here is an example of how to be open to people's feelings when you ask a question:

Imagine that you are having a wonderful time on your new roller derby team and you want to ask a new teammate how they like the team so far:

1.     Start with a neutral question like, "Do you like roller derby so far?" rather than, "Isn't roller derby awesome?" Keep an open mind about how your teammate might answer. If your teammate can sense that you want them to say yes, they might feel pressured to answer that way.

2.     If your teammate shares that they are not having fun on the team, listen and accept their answer. Don't try to argue with a statement like, "How can you not love the team?" or "But you looked like you were having fun!"

3.     If you ask your teammate why they don't like roller derby, make sure your tone indicates that you just want to learn why they don't like it, not that you are criticizing them for how they feel. You could also ask a more specific question, such as, "Is it the sport itself that you don't like, or do you not like this particular team?" If your teammate just doesn't like the sport, that's fine. But it's also possible that your teammate enjoys the sport but feels excluded from the group, and that making more of an effort to include them would make all the difference. Be open to both responses. Sometimes you can make changes that will improve a situation for someone, and other times it's just not a good fit.

4.     Remember that it is okay for people to like different things, so the fact that someone else doesn't like the roller derby team does not mean that the team has to be any less awesome for you.

## "How Are You?"

There is one question that most of us ask every day, despite not being open to a variety of responses: "How are you?" People expect everyone to say that they are good, but everyone is not always feeling well. If you are required to say "Hi, how are you?" to people as part of your job, it is perfectly fine if you don't want to engage with everyone on a deeper level. But when you are speaking with people you know and care about – or people you want to get to know – this question does not always have to be a formality. If you sincerely care about someone, then "How are you?" can be a sincere question. When you ask, "How are you?" in a formal greeting tone, people may automatically answer that they are good. Whereas if you use a more sincere tone, you are inviting the person to open up to you. Think of the way that you would ask, "How have you been feeling?" if you knew that someone had been sick. This is a good tone to use when you ask people how they are doing. It doesn't mean you are assuming that anything is wrong – it just shows that you are open to the possibility of them not being good.

Here are some example of validating and invalidating responses when someone tells you that they are not feeling well:
Invalidating responses:
"Aww, come on, it can't be that bad!"
"Aren't you over that by now?"
"You're just thinking too much about it."
"How can you be sad on such a nice sunny day like this?"
Validating responses:
"What's wrong?"
"Wow, that sounds like a really stressful week!"
"Is there anything that would make you feel better?"
"Do you want a hug?"
[Just listen until they are finished talking]

Finally, when you actively encourage someone to share with you – or if you know something is wrong and assure someone that they can talk to you – you need to take what they say seriously. When someone is afraid to talk about a problem, it is often because they are worried about how other people will react. If you tell someone that they can talk to you, *you need to be prepared to follow through and validate their feelings.* Being prepared to follow through doesn't mean that you have to solve all of the person's problems. It does not mean that if your friend is stressed out about an upcoming exam, you are obligated to help them study. It *does* mean that you are willing to listen to how stressed out your friend is and not tell them that they are overthinking things, not tell them that the issue is less of a big deal than they are making it out to be, and not say anything like, "That's ALL?" When someone opens up to you, they are putting a lot of trust in you, so invalidating their feelings after you've said that they could talk to you is a betrayal of trust.

# That's Embarrassing!

Embarrassment is a bit of a tricky emotion. The normal rule of validation is to take everything as seriously as the person in the situation is taking it, but when someone feels embarrassed, they are often happy to hear that an incident is not as significant as it feels. It may be reassuring to know that no one is going to remember or care about their mishap for very long.

Your friend might want reassurance, but they also might want to never hear about the incident again.

If, for example, your friend was mortified because they threw up in front of everyone yesterday, when you see your friend again, you could just ask them, "Are you feeling better?" or "How are you feeling?" the same way you would any other time that your friend is sick. If your friend doesn't bring up the subject of throwing up, you shouldn't either. Let your friend move on. *If* your friend says, "I can't believe I threw up in front of everyone!" you can validate their feelings while also assuring them that it is not a big deal. You could say something validating like, "That must have been hard," but also reassure them with something like, "It's okay. It happens to everyone," or "Don't worry, everyone's already forgotten about it by now," or "Think about how you'd react if someone else threw up. It wouldn't stay in your mind forever, would it?" Your friend might feel relieved to hear these things and change the subject. Let the person who got embarrassed make the decision to bring up the subject of what happened and how long they want to discuss it. If they don't bring up the subject, don't mention it.

When someone is embarrassed, look for ways that you can help them subtly, without drawing more attention to them. You do not want to ask someone, "Are you embarrassed?" the same way that you would ask if they are worried or upset. Bringing up the fact that they are embarrassed will probably make them feel even *more* embarrassed. If someone falls and spills their lunch in front of everyone, help them out and ask if they are okay, then drop the subject. If they seem like they want to move on, don't keep fussing over them.

In situations where a person might be embarrassed, pay attention to the person's feelings and respond accordingly. Imagine that you and your friends are going around naming your favorite TV shows. When Mariela names her favorite show, everyone else laughs and says that her favorite show is for babies. Now, this might be a good time for you to

44

stick up for Mariela, but depending on the situation, Mariela might be so mortified that she just wants everyone's attention directed somewhere else. Pay attention to how Mariela reacts: If Mariela seems annoyed or angry, or if she fights back for herself and says that there is nothing wrong with the show she likes, it would be a good opportunity to stand up for Mariela. But if, on the other hand, Mariela looks totally mortified, like she *never* would have said anything if she'd known how everyone else would react – or worse, if watching this show was Mariela's secret and someone else told the group – Mariela probably will not want all of the extra attention that would come from you standing up for her and prolonging the issue. In this case, you might be better off making a brief comment – for instance, making a joke or saying something positive about the TV show – and then changing the subject to get the attention off of Mariela. While it's great to stand up for your friends, it's also important to recognize when someone doesn't want attention on themself, and to help get them out of the spotlight.

# That's Private!

Being embarrassed is not the only reason that someone might not want your validation to be loud or public. Sometimes, privacy is more important. If a friend tells you that something is private, do not bring up that topic around other people. If you think your friend *might* want to keep something private, even if they didn't specifically tell you, it is better not to bring up that topic in front of people. For instance, don't ask your friend at a group event, "So, how did your medical test turn out?" Don't publically mention that your friend just lost their job unless they bring up the subject first. You can always just ask your friend, "How are you doing?" and let them decide how much they want to share with everyone. If you don't have a minute alone with your friend, you can always call, email, or text your friend to see how they are doing or offer to talk to them in private.

Be mindful of whether or not someone has chosen to share something potentially private with you. For example, if someone has to take medicine while you're around, or miss time from school or work because they have doctor's appointments, that person did not necessarily *choose* to share that information with you. While it's alright to ask, "Is everything okay?" if you are concerned about someone, be sure to respect their boundaries if they do not want to share details.

Keep confidentiality in mind when you communicate on social media as well. If you find a great article about an issue that your friend has dealt with personally – such as living with a disorder or overcoming a past trauma – send it to your friend in an email or private message rather than in a place where others can see it, unless your friend has explicitly told you that it is okay to share those things publically. Even while expressing legitimate concern for others, be sure to respect their privacy.

There are also times when a person just does not want any attention drawn to themself or what they are doing. If you are eating dinner with your family and your partner, and you notice that your partner is just picking at their food, it's not necessarily a good idea to ask them, "Is the spaghetti okay?" in front of everyone. While you are trying to be considerate, you are actually putting your partner on the spot. You are drawing everyone's attention to the fact that they are not eating much, when they might have been hoping that no one would notice. Most people in their position would not be comfortable saying,

"No, I don't like this spaghetti sauce," in front of your parents. A better way to handle that situation is to not say anything. If you are concerned that your partner might still be hungry, you can put out a snack later that you know they like. While it's great to check in on someone to make sure that they are doing okay, it is also good to understand when giving them attention in front of others may cause more problems.

# But What if Someone *Really* Won't Stop Complaining?

Now, you might be wondering, what if someone just won't stop complaining about something? What if they are going on and on about the same thing and you really feel like telling them to get over it? What if you really feel like they should be happy and are just focusing on the negative part of the situation?

Imagine that you and your friends all had a wonderful day at the amusement park, but on the ride home, one of your friends is complaining about something bad that happened to them. Their feet hurt, they got a bad sunburn, they felt left out of the group, etc. Their complaining is bothering you. You wish they would focus on all the awesome fun things that they did that day instead of just focusing on the one thing that went wrong.

1.      Think about *why* their complaining is bothering you so much. If you are tired from the long day and just aren't up for being supportive, it would be fine to let your friend know that you are too tired to discuss it. It's okay to know that your friend could use more support *and* that you're not up to giving it. Both of those things can be true, and it doesn't have to mean that either of you is being a bad friend. On the other hand, if the complaining bothers you because you think your friend is just being negative and needs to change their attitude in order to feel better, remember that complaining arises from a real need. Validating your friend's feelings will *ease* the pain, whereas invalidating them will make it worse.

2.      Listen. Clear your mind of how you *think* your friend should feel right now, and really listen to what they are telling you. You may have *thought* your friend was having a great day, but the problem they are telling you about may have been affecting them the entire time. They may have avoided mentioning it earlier in an attempt to be polite and not spoil everyone else's good time. The fact that your friend is just mentioning the problem now, at the end of the day, does not necessarily mean that it was not affecting them all day long.

3.      If it's true that your friend did not have a fun day at all because of this issue, remember that everyone likes different things, and it is okay if you had a wonderful day and your friend did not. If something about the trip could have been done differently, you can use this information to be more accommodating to your friend in the future. You can make more of an effort to include everyone, and you can make sure

to ask, "What rides does everyone want to go on?" and "Does anyone want to take a break?" But if the amusement park trip was just not your friend's cup of tea, that is also okay. After you talk to your friend about what the problem was, you'll have a better understanding of what they like and dislike, and your friend may have a better understanding of their own interests as well.

4.      If, after listening closely, it sounds like your friend did have fun earlier and is complaining about something that did *not* ruin their entire day, you can accept their feelings anyway. If you don't want to spend the whole three-hour car ride home talking about how much your friend's feet hurt, just say, "That's annoying!" or "Aw man, I hate it when that happens!" and ask if there is anything that might help. Perhaps an ice-cold soda can from the cooler would soothe your friend's sore feet.

5.      If you know that your friend did have fun at the amusement park and you want to change the subject back to that, you can do so without trying to lessen your friend's problem. If your friend has been complaining about something, instead of saying, "But you still had fun on the rides, right?" you could wait for a break in the conversation and say something like, "I loved the new roller coaster! What was your favorite ride?" Your friend may tell you about their favorite ride and be reminded of how much fun they had. You will be *inviting* them to remember the happier parts of the day, rather than pushing them.

6.      If you try to change the subject and your friend still just wants to complain, let them be and do not push them to feel differently. Some people just focus on one thing at a time, and the negative feelings that they are experiencing right now might be too overwhelming for them to think about anything else. If your friend really did have a fun day, then they had a fun day. That positive experience will not get erased just because your friend isn't up for talking about their favorite rides at the moment. If you check back with your friend tomorrow or in a week's time, they may tell you that they loved riding the bumper cars and the Ferris Wheel and spending the day with their friends. But for now, whatever they are feeling is fine.

# When You Don't Agree

We've established what to do when your friend has a problem that matters more to them than to you. But what do you do when you think your friend is wrong about what happened? What if your friend is upset because of something that someone else did to them, but as an outside observer, you think that what happened was a mistake or a misunderstanding? Here is an example:

Friend: "I cannot believe this – I posted on Facebook that my gerbil died, and my best friend hasn't even responded! It was a whole hour ago! He doesn't care about me anymore!"

Response A: "He probably just hasn't seen your status yet. Everyone isn't glued to the Internet all the time."

Response B: "I'm so sorry that your gerbil died. Your best friend should respond, but he may not have seen your status yet. He could be busy right now. Maybe you could try contacting him directly and giving him some time to respond."

Even though both responses express the same interpretation of what happened – that your friend's best friend did not see the Facebook status – the second response is much better because:

1.     You validated your friend's feelings first. You acknowledged how bad your friend must feel, and how bad it *would* feel to have his best friend not care about him. Remember, your friend is reacting to what he *thinks* happened, even though you can see that he might have misunderstood.

2.     You offered your opinion in an understanding way. Response A makes it sound like your friend is being silly and that you are defending his best friend, but Response B shows that you understand that your friend is upset and might have misinterpreted what happened. Remember: feelings themselves are not wrong, even if they are based on a misunderstanding.

It's one thing to have a misunderstanding. But what do you do when you actually don't agree with what your friend is saying? What if your friend is fuming after an argument they had with someone, but you find yourself taking the side of the other person?

For example: Your friend Chrystal got into a fight with her friend Latisha because Chrystal was expecting Latisha to do something for her – something that Latisha did not want to do, but Chrystal expected of her because they are friends. When you hear about this argument, you find yourself taking Latisha's side because you don't believe that Latisha owes this favor to Chrystal. How do you validate Chrystal when you just don't agree with her side of the argument?

1.      Listen. Your opinion is perfectly valid, but Chrystal might not be looking for an opinion just yet. Let Chrystal vent to you about the fight without taking sides in the fight yourself. The act of explaining the situation to someone else might help Chrystal understand what went wrong, and figure out how to resolve the conflict on her own.

2.      Validate your friend's feelings even if you disagree. Feelings and desires are not wrong. It is perfectly fine for Chrystal to *want* Latisha to do something for her, and it is okay for her to feel upset about not getting what she wants. Whether Latisha actually owed Chrystal this favor is a separate issue.

3.      After Chrystal has vented to you and calmed down a bit, you can ask her if she wants your advice or opinion, and offer it gently.

4.      Advise communication. You may be sitting there thinking that Latisha doesn't owe Chrystal this favor, so Chrystal should just drop it, but since the problem started with Chrystal not understanding Latisha's boundaries, it won't really be resolved until Chrystal and Latisha have a full discussion about what their boundaries are.

When you find yourself taking the side of the other person in an argument, it can be difficult to discuss the issue with your friend in a way that validates their feelings. After listening and letting them vent to you, advising that they discuss the problem with the other person involved is often a good move. Unless your friend really did something wrong to the other person – such as bullying or threatening them – think of the conflict as an incompatibility between two people. Conflicts arise when people disagree on the expectations within their relationships, which is why Crystal and Latisha had a fight, and why they need to discuss their boundaries. Encouraging this communication validates the existence of the problem without being dishonest about whose side you are on.

We've gone over what to do when you don't agree with a friend's opinion. But what do you do when you don't agree with a friend's *decision*?

Imagine that you and your friend are on a sports team together. Some of your teammates make fun of your friend for being slow and uncoordinated. After a while, your friend tells you that they are quitting the team because they don't want to deal with the bullying anymore. You know that teasing feels bad, but you just don't see this as a good enough reason to quit the team. How do you respond to your friend's decision?

First of all, ask yourself *why* you are opposed to your friend's decision. Are you worried that your friend will regret their decision later because they love the sport? Or are you thinking that getting teased is just not a good enough reason to quit and that your friend should find a way to stick it out?

If you are worried about your friend regretting their own decision, let them know that it is understandable that they would want to quit the team, and then ask them gently, "Are you sure that you want to quit? You love hockey, and it's a shame to have to give up something you care about." See how they respond. You can also offer to help, such going with your friend to discuss the bullying with your coach.

If you just think that the bullying is not a good enough reason to quit, you need to respect your friend's decision and not pressure them to choose differently. Validation means accepting that if your friend says the bullying is bad enough for them to quit the team, it is bad enough for them to quit the team, even if you would never quit for the same reason, and even if you think that it's wrong to quit for that reason. If your friend decides to quit, respect their choice.

Validation means letting other people make the choices that are right for them. But what do you do if someone's decision is going to hurt others? How can you validate a friend's feelings when they want to do something harmful?

Imagine that your friend Justin comes to you, fuming because his friend Mike broke a special vase that Justin's grandmother gave to him before she died. Mike knew how much the vase meant to Justin, but in a game of truth or dare at Justin's party, someone dared Mike to sneak into Justin's room and smash the vase with a baseball bat, and Mike went along with the dare just to show off to his friends. "What a traitor!" Justin tells you, "Next time I'm at Mike's house, I wanna break something special of his in front of all his friends, so he'll know what it feels like!" You know that it's wrong for Justin to destroy Mike's belongings in this way. How do you let Justin know that this behavior would not be acceptable, while still validating his feelings?

1.      Feelings first. You can still be understanding of the way someone feels without supporting them hurting others. Your wording here is very important. What Mike did is bad enough for Justin to *feel* like he wants to destroy Mike's most prized possessions. The fact that Justin shouldn't actually break Mike's stuff is a separate issue. So *before* telling Justin that his plan is not okay, validate his feelings the same way you would if he hadn't mentioned breaking Mike's things. Say, "Wow, Mike completely violated your trust!" "I can't believe he would do such a thing!" "You must be feeling so bad right now!" "Did you talk to Mike about how you feel?" "Is there anything that would make you feel better right now? Do you feel like hanging out and talking or doing something that you enjoy?" It's possible that Justin is making this threat right now because he is angry, and after talking it out with you, he will not actually carry out this plan. He may decide not to take any action. He may decide to confront Mike verbally. Be open to discussing these choices with Justin, and give him the chance to decide on his own that he is not going to break Mike's things.

2.      If, after you have validated Justin's feelings and talked about the problem or given him a chance to cool down, he still talks about wanting to break Mike's possessions, you can let him know that you don't think that is acceptable. Make sure you indicate that you understand how serious the issue is, but that breaking Mike's belongings would be unacceptable *despite* that. If you imply that breaking Mike's stuff is unacceptable because the situation *isn't bad enough*, then Justin might feel like you're denying how much he feels hurt by it. And then he might be *more* motivated to do something drastic, to prove how upset it really made him. So, instead, make it clear that you think the issue *is* very important, and offer to help Justin come up with a different solution.

3.      One common mistake people make in this situation is that they suggest a course of action that comes nowhere near what the person originally wanted to do.  This is a form of invalidation. Just as it's invalidating to call someone else's problem "inconvenient" when they have referred to it as "a nightmare," it's invalidating to suggest that your friend should walk away or not take any action when they clearly want to react to the problem. A solution only "works" if it works for the individual. A lot of people advise others to ignore acts of meanness and walk away, but this solution only works if it both stops the mean acts

*and* makes the person feel better. Ignoring Mike's actions and moving on might not be a solution that will work for Justin.

A possible solution in this case could be for Justin to ban Mike from future parties at his house. This would be a perfectly acceptable choice, and it would also involve Mike having to face the consequences of his actions, which is what Justin wanted in the first place. Justin could also talk to Mike about what he did wrong and how hurtful his actions were. Justin can explain that he felt betrayed when Mike was willing to break something precious to him just to show off to their other friends. This could give Mike a chance to apologize and accept responsibility for his actions.

When we hear that someone wants to do something hurtful, we often have an initial instinct to stop them by telling them that they are taking things too far. Next time someone tells you that they want to do something hurtful, listen closely to what they're saying, to what they really want, and see if you can find an alternative, non-hurtful solution that would still achieve the result that they're looking for.

# Part 2: Common Forms of Invalidation

# But Some People Just Cause Drama!

When people are having a conflict, other people sometimes write it off by calling it "drama." "Drama" can involve serious conflicts between people, but the term can also imply that someone is making a big deal over nothing. The trouble with callings things "drama" is that the term encompasses a wide range of conflicts – both conflicts that do not need to exist, and existing conflicts that do need to be addressed.

Imagine that someone says to a group of people, "Can you believe that Zoe wore the same sweater three days in a row?" Now, the fact that Zoe wore the same sweater for three days is not a problem. Zoe's sweater is not hurting anybody. The fact that someone announced this to the group is an example of creating a conflict over nothing. However, referring to this incident as "drama" can also downplay how hurt Zoe might be by this gossip when she hears about it. Furthermore, if Zoe hears about this gossip and later says to the group, "I'm not okay with you making fun of my clothes, and I'd like you to stop," Zoe is not creating a conflict out of thin air – she is *addressing* a conflict that already exists. If you lump all conflict together as "drama," it can make it difficult to distinguish between creating conflict and addressing conflict. People in Zoe's position are often accused of "causing drama" when they are in fact responding to conflicts that already exist.

Sometimes, when you think someone is "causing drama," it is because you cannot see the conflict that already exists. Sometimes *you* may feel afraid to speak up about something that is hurting you because you don't want to "cause drama." But if you or someone else is being hurt by something, there is already a conflict.

Imagine this scenario: You're having a quiet day at home when your friend Keisha calls and asks if you can take care of her cat, Max, for the week. You love cats, so you tell Keisha that she can bring Max over right away. But Max is ferocious. As soon as Keisha drops him off, Max starts terrorizing your home. He claws your furniture to shreds, scratches every inch of the walls, and tries to devour every piece of clothing in your closet. If you make any attempt to stop Max, he bites or scratches you. When you consider telling Keisha that you can't take care of Max after all, your first thought is that you don't want to create a conflict with her. But when you look around the room at all your books that have been ripped apart and clothes that have been shredded to pieces, you realize that you already have a conflict. Having Max in your home *is* a conflict. Telling Keisha that you can't do the job anymore is not creating a problem out of nowhere. You *have* a problem. It's just contained in your home, where Keisha can't see it.

The same is true no matter what is bothering you. Maybe you feel betrayed because your friends ignored you while you were going through a crisis. Maybe it hurts you when your family and friends refuse to use your correct pronouns. Or maybe it just bothers you when your parents always nag you to get a "better" job when you're content with the job you have. Whatever is hurting you *is a problem.*

When the pain is internal, you can't see the problem as clearly as you could see what Max had done to your home in the above example. When you feel bad and want to say something but you're afraid of causing conflict, remind yourself that what's going on inside you is real, even if other people can't see it.

The same is true for everyone around you. Anyone can have problems that they haven't talked about, problems that you cannot necessarily see. When someone says that something you did upset them or made them feel bad in some way, it can be natural to deny it or claim that the conflict doesn't exist. When you can't see the conflict, it feels like it isn't there. But remember: Keisha couldn't see what her cat was doing to your home. If you care about someone, you should invite them to share how they are feeling. And people who care about you should invite you to share how you are feeling.

See if you can identify which of these statements involve the speaker causing conflict, and which ones involve the speaker addressing a conflict that already exists:

1. "I can't be seen with you in public if you're going to dress that way!"
2. "Paul hasn't spoken to me in a week, and I'm worried he doesn't like me anymore!"
3. "Neetu told me that she has a crush on Laura, but I overheard Laura say that she doesn't like Neetu and she plans to ask Brianna out!"
4. "I'm angry that you told my secret to the whole family!"
5. "That TV show is for babies! I can't believe you still watch it!"
6. "Please don't take my stuff without asking!"
7. "You can't be friends with anyone that I don't approve of!"
8. "If you don't stop harassing me, I'm going to report you!"

Answer: The odd-numbered choices involve the speaker creating a conflict, and the even-numbered choices involve the speaker addressing a conflict that already exists.

1. Unless this person is wearing magical clothes that put a curse on anyone who touches them, their clothes are not causing a problem, even if other people disapprove of them. Insulting their clothing is creating a problem.

2. If you are worried that someone doesn't like you or is upset with you, that is a problem. Even if it turns out that Paul is just busy or preoccupied this week, the fact that you feel bad makes it an existing conflict. However, to avoid creating further conflict, it would be better to address this with Paul directly instead of telling a lot of other people.

3. While a potential conflict exists in this case, it is between the people involved. Passing on gossip like this can create more trouble.

4. If someone else told your secret to your whole family, *they* created a conflict. Sharing how you feel about their behavior is reacting to an existing problem.

5. It is a not a problem that you and another person have different tastes. Putting them down for what they like is creating a conflict.

6. Asking people to respect your boundaries is reacting to an existing or potential conflict. Also, if your friends care about your feelings and thought that you were okay with them borrowing your things without asking, asserting your boundaries could prevent their behavior from turning into a bigger problem.

7. You do not have the right to decide who someone else can choose as friends. Your friend choosing their own friends is not a problem, and trying to control their behavior will create a problem.

8. If someone is harassing you, that is an existing problem. Threatening to report the person is a justifiable way of protecting yourself.

When we lump everything together as "drama," we can easily end up shutting people down who are trying to discuss existing problems. A good step towards validating everyone's feelings is to replace the word "drama" with "conflict." "Drama" automatically implies that someone is making something out of nothing, whereas "conflict" implies a legitimate issue. Having a "drama-free" community may sound nice, but it could also make people feel like they can't speak up if they have a problem, for fear that they will be labeled as "causing drama." If you change the word "drama" to "conflict," you realize that a "conflict-free" community would be unrealistic. A community can never be free from all conflict. Try replacing the word "drama" with more specific things that you don't want, such as bullying, mean gossip, exclusion, and betrayal. Instead of trying to eliminate all conflict, aim to build a community of respect and mutual trust, where everyone feels safe talking about their feelings.

# No Comparison

One of the most important parts of validation is to focus on what a person is feeling without comparing their situation to anyone else's. A common way that we invalidate people's feelings is by comparing their situations to others. This can happen in all sorts of ways.

## Bigger Issues

Maybe someone tells you that your problems are not actually that bad because other people have it worse or because there are bigger problems in the world. This is extremely invalidating because it tells people, "You shouldn't feel this bad," or worse, "You don't have a right to feel this bad over this problem." It's your life, your situation, and your feelings. Whatever importance you place on something, that's how important it is, no matter how it compares to other problems in the world. The same is true of everyone else. If someone indicates that something is of a certain importance, that is how important it is. If someone indicates that something in their life is extremely bad, problematic, or just not acceptable to live with, then that is exactly how that thing is. If you like to make *yourself* feel better by putting your problems into perspective, that is perfectly fine, but it is not okay to use bigger issues to invalidate other people's problems unless they have specifically asked you to do so.

Maybe your friend posts on Facebook, "I hate it here! I'd rather be ANYWHERE than here!!!" and your instinct is to comment and tell them that there are lots of worse places. Remember that although what your friend said might not be factually true, it is emotionally true. Whatever is going on right now is bad enough for your friend to *feel* like they would rather be anywhere else, and that feeling is legitimate, regardless of whether they would literally opt to be absolutely anywhere else in the world. Criticizing their choice of words will invalidate their feelings. Instead, focus your attention on the actual problem. It's not about all the other worse places that your friend could be – it's about where they are now.

## Generation Gaps

No matter how old you are right now, you have things that you rely on, and things that are an important part of your life, that your parents did not have when they were your age. Now ask yourself: Does the fact that your parents did not have these things at your age mean that you would be willing to live without them now? And I don't mean going back to your parents' time – I mean, if the rest of the world stayed the same and everyone around you had the same technology that they do now, would you feel perfectly fine giving up everything that your parents didn't have when they were the age that you are now?

The same is true for younger generations. The world is a constantly changing place, and even if you lived without something at their age, that does not mean that they should be willing or able to do the same. If you didn't grow up with a cell phone or Internet access, that does not make it a less valid problem when a person is upset about not having those things today, or getting them taken away as a punishment. Not having access to a cell phone or the Internet creates more limitations on someone's life today than it would have years ago. If you grew up playing outside with kids in your neighborhood and didn't have a lot of technology, it may be hard to relate to someone who is upset about losing something that you were happy without. But nowadays, that child might not have a bunch of neighborhood friends that they can just go out and play with. Their primary form of communication and entertainment might be on their cell phone or computer, and taking those things away might be the equivalent of not being able to leave your bedroom when you were younger. The Internet allows people to connect with others who share their interests and their life experiences. For example, if you are the only person in your town who has autism, you might be able to meet other people who have autism in online communities, discuss your shared experiences, feel less alone, and as a result, have a better quality of life than you might have had before you had the opportunity to connect with others in this way. Cutting someone off from a support system such as this could be traumatic. Instead of thinking, "But when I was ten, I didn't have a cell phone!" think, "How would I feel if someone took away my phone *now*?" Because it is now. It's not the world that it was when you were ten.

Additionally, the fact that something was more socially acceptable in the past (for example, bullying or corporal punishment) does not mean that it was ever okay. Even if no one complained about something back when you were younger, that does not mean that it never hurt anyone, or that no one needed the resources that we have now. Even if someone never spoke about an issue, that does not mean that it never affected them. If someone says that something is a problem for them now, it is a problem now. The fact that people didn't take the problem seriously in the past *is a problem with the past,* not an excuse to invalidate the person now.

## Different Reactions

Maybe your friend is complaining that they are way too busy, when you are busier than they are and don't complain about it. Maybe lots of people you know are much busier than your friend is and don't complain about it. Maybe what your friend is doing is not even what most people would consider to be "busy." That's okay. This does not mean that your friend is lying or exaggerating. It means that your friend is not okay with the same activity level in their life that you are in yours. Complaining about something means that you don't like it, and it is perfectly normal for people to have different likes and dislikes. Just as it's perfectly normal for one person to complain about the cafeteria hot dogs while another person raves over them, it's also perfectly normal for some people to like being busy, or least be okay with being busy, and for others to hate it. No matter how many people are busier than your friend, their complaint is completely valid. Talk to them the *same way* you would if they *did* have so much going on that you would consider them to be too busy.

The same is true for positive things. If your friend is really proud of themself for something that everyone wouldn't necessarily see as a big deal, such as getting to work on time, getting their homework done on time, going for a short walk, or even just getting out of bed on a day when it was difficult for them, congratulate them and let them feel good about themself. Focus on your friend's feelings without comparing their situation to anyone else's.

Also, keep in mind that staying quiet about a problem does not make someone a better person than someone who complains about the problem. It is easy to say, "So what? Other people have that problem and they're not complaining," but everyone has different reactions to things, and the fact that some people do not complain about things does not revoke other people's right to complain. Avoid saying things like, "Isabella's parents got divorced too, but she's over it now. Why aren't you over it?" Or, "Isabella's parents got divorced too, but you don't see her crying all the time/complaining to everyone online/acting the way you're acting." Every person's experience is unique, and the fact that your friend is behaving differently than other people who have had the same experience is fine and does not make their feelings any less legitimate.

Everyone has different reactions to things: Some people complain and some people keep their troubles private. Some people have big reactions and some people have more subtle reactions. Some people show everyone exactly how they are feeling and some people look the same on the outside. Some people get worse at all their other tasks when they are having a problem, and some people compartmentalize their problems. Even if other people in worse situations are not reacting the same way as your friend, that has absolutely nothing to do with your friend. Validation means treating each person's experience as unique, focusing in on their problem, and not comparing their situation to anything else.

## But What if *I'm* Dealing with Something Bigger?

I once got a disturbing phone call from a friend. She told me that while she was visiting her brother at his college, he had a medical emergency and no one in his dorm would help. She ran around the dorm pleading for help, and everyone just ignored her. She called an ambulance, and her brother ended up being okay. After I got off the phone with my friend, I was very shaken. I just couldn't fathom how all those students did not care about their classmate. About twenty minutes later, I was lying in bed, still replaying the conversation with my friend and visualizing the scene of what happened, when my phone rang again. It was a different friend. I don't normally answer the phone when I'm not up for talking, but because of what had just happened, I couldn't help thinking, *What if it's an emergency?* So, I answered the phone, and my second friend, who sounded like she had been crying, whispered, "I had a fight with my mom." I didn't know what to say. My mind felt frozen. I was still trying to process the fact that my friend's brother almost died and no one in his dorm cared. I needed to talk to someone about that before I could engage in a conversation about something else.

64

And yet, my second friend had called me to get support, so I didn't feel that I could tell her why I was upset. I did the wrong thing in this case – I basically froze up and didn't engage with my friend at all, not even asking her about the fight, and she got off the phone thinking that I didn't care. Looking back on it, I should have let her know that I did care, that I did want to talk to her, but I just wasn't feeling well enough to talk at that moment and I would call her back the next day.

Sometimes, you will be bogged down with bigger issues than what your friends are talking to you about, and you won't be able to give them your full attention and support. That is okay. You need to take care of yourself. The important thing is that you let them know that you aren't feeling well, and focus on how you're not up for engaging, rather than focusing on how their problems are less significant than yours.

For example: Imagine that your grandfather just passed away during your spring vacation, and you haven't told anyone the news yet. On your first day back, a friend comes up to you and starts complaining that their spring break was ruined because their teacher assigned way too much homework. Try your best not to snap at your friend that there are bigger issues. You could try saying something like, "I'm not feeling very well right now. My grandfather died over spring break, and I've been having a really difficult time." This puts the focus on *yourself*, rather than criticizing your friend for complaining about homework when you had a death in the family. Most likely, your friend will automatically stop complaining and offer you support. If your friend cares about you, they will probably say, "I'm so sorry! I didn't realize that!" and turn the conversation to you. *If* they continue to complain about their homework and seem to want your support when you just can't give it, let them know that you're not feeling well enough to talk about it. Alternatively, if you don't want to share what is wrong, you could just let your friend know that you're not feeling well and have been having a rough time, but you aren't up for talking about what happened. As long as you keep the focus on yourself and your own needs, you will avoid invalidating your friend, and your friend should offer you support.

## Past, Present, Future: It Matters Now

### "Aren't You Over That by Now?"

Imagine that you're standing around, minding your own business, when someone comes along and pushes you down the stairs. You break your leg from the fall. The next week, you're on crutches and unable to do most of your normal activities. When you tell your friends that this person pushed you down the stairs, their reaction is, "That happened a whole week ago! Why aren't you walking on your leg again? Aren't you over it by now?" Doesn't this reaction sound silly? You may have gotten pushed down the stairs a week ago, but your leg is still clearly broken! You will probably be on crutches for at least a few months. To say that the injury happened in the past is irrelevant because it is clearly affecting you right now. Furthermore, this injury can continue to affect your life even after the cast comes off. If you have a job that requires physical labor, for example, you could be out of work for a long time while your leg is broken. If you play on a sports team, you could miss tryouts or be out for the season. All of the things that you weren't able to do while your leg was broken can still have an impact on your life once your leg is healed.

The trouble with emotional pain is that we can't see it as clearly as a physical injury. If you fall down the stairs, everyone can see that your leg is still in a cast several weeks later. But if you get hurt emotionally, people can't see the emotional injury the way they can see a broken leg. It becomes all too easy to act like an incident should no longer be affecting someone because it happened in the past. When someone is talking about a situation from the past as if it is still happening, *it is still happening*. When you tell someone to just get over something that hurt them emotionally in the past, it is no different than telling someone that their leg can't still be broken.

How do you validate someone's past experience? Treat their experience the way that they do. If your friend is talking about something that happened a long time ago as if it happened yesterday – a breakup, a death in the family, a traumatic experience, etc. – talk to them about it as if it happened yesterday. Discuss it with them the same way you would discuss something that happened more recently, because it *is* recent to them. Understand that whatever happened is still very important to your friend and is affecting them deeply. And accept the choices that your friend makes based on their past experiences. If your friend says that they never want to visit a particular place again or see a particular person again because of something that happened many years ago, that is totally fine. Accept their decisions and do not push them to do those things. Understand that sometimes people shut out the pain while an event is happening, so even if a traumatic experience happened several years ago, this could be the first time that the person is processing their emotions and talking about what happened. Emotional events can feel much more recent if someone blocked out their feelings at the time and are just now beginning to share.

If your friend keeps talking about the same thing over and over again, even years after it has happened, and do not remind them of how much time has passed. Don't say, "But that happened three years ago, right?" or worse, "Aren't you over that by now?" If you personally are tired of hearing the same story over and over, you can tell your friend that you are not emotionally up for it, but focus on yourself not being up for the conversation, rather than focusing on how long your friend spends talking about the issue. You can also segue into a different subject and see if your friend is receptive to it. But do not pressure your friend to be over something that they are not over. If your friend is still talking about something now, then the emotional injury still exists now.

### "See? You Had Nothing to Worry About!"

Imagine that you have to cross your neighbor's yard, but they have a pet alligator that might attack you. You approach the yard with apprehension, only to find the alligator asleep in its cage. While it is true that you *no longer* have anything to worry about, you *did* have something to worry about a moment earlier, when you didn't know where the alligator would be. When someone is worried about something that ends up being a non-issue, the person had no way of knowing in advance that everything would be okay. Instead of saying, "See! There was nothing to worry about!" a more validating response could be, "That must have been really scary not knowing what was going to happen! I'm glad that things turned out well."

## "This Won't Matter in Ten Years!"

Older people often tell younger people, "This won't matter five years from now," or "You won't remember any of this in ten years." Phrases like this are invalidating and condescending on a number of levels. The first problem is these statements attempt to lessen the importance of something that is going on right now. Instead of saying, "This shouldn't matter as much now because it happened in the past," you are saying, "This shouldn't matter as much now because it will not matter in the future." None of us can know for sure what will happen in the future, but even if you *did* have some way to know that it would not matter in the future, that would not change how much something is affecting a person right now. Now, if someone is *worried* about the future, for instance, if a child asks, "Will I *always* get picked on for being the shortest kid in my class?" then it's fine to assure them that their problem will not go on forever. But if they are only talking about how they feel right now, then you should only be discussing the current issue. What matters to someone now matters period, regardless of what will happen tomorrow or a year from now.

Secondly, you do not necessarily know what a person will remember when they are older, or how they will feel about those memories. You may not remember or care about things that happened to you five or ten years ago, but that does not mean that everyone else will feel the same way. You may have experienced being a particular age, but you do not know what someone else's experience of the age will be. They are different from you, and the world will be a different place for them by the time they are your age.

Most of the adults who told me that I would not remember things, or that I would not care about them in five or ten years, were wrong. I do still remember most things that I was told I would forget, and a lot of things still matter to me that people told me would not matter. You can never know what another person will remember or what will still matter to them.

In any case, something does not *need* to matter in the future in order for it to matter now. We do not need psychological research on the long-term damage of anything in order to know that it is hurting someone right now. Even if you somehow knew with 100% certainty that a problem would not affect someone when they were older and that they would still "turn out" okay, it would still be a problem because it is hurting the person right now.

## "This Is the Best Time of Your Life!"

There is a flip-side of telling people that things won't matter in five or ten years, and that is telling people that certain things definitely *will* still matter in five or ten years. In my high school, lots of people said that prom night would be the best night of our lives. And people often say that college will be the best four years of your life. While these are positive sentiments, they put a lot of unnecessary stress on people who do not enjoy these times. When everyone insists on prom being one of the best nights of your life, it puts a lot of pressure on people to have a perfect night. This includes people who are not interested in prom, as well as people who are just not able to have the prom of their dreams. While it's fine to enjoy prom, it's better not to assume that other people will, or should, have prom be the best night of their lives. If someone has an unpleasant prom experience – or no prom experience – it will not feel good to be told that it was supposed to be the best night of their entire life.

It's common for older people to tell younger people which years will be the best years of their lives – childhood years, teen years, or college years, for instance. If you personally enjoyed a particular time of your life, that's great. But when you try to tell other people which years of *their* lives will be the best, you can actually end up hurting them. It may seem like a nice thing to tell someone that they are in their best time of their life, or that they are about to enter it, but the fact is, this time may *not* be the best time of that person's life. You don't know what the person is experiencing. They could be going through a very difficult time and hoping that it will end soon. Think of the worst experience of your life so far. Now, think of how you would feel if, when you told someone how terrible you felt, they told you that what you were going through was the best experience of your life and that you should enjoy it while you have the chance. While it is meant to be a positive sentiment, telling someone that they are in the best time of their life when they are having a bad time is actually very depressing. Going to college was the worst experience of my life, yet I was constantly being bombarded with messages of, "College is the best four years of your life." This attitude towards college hurt me deeply. I

69

thought the fact that I hated college would follow me for my entire life, since everyone would continue to refer to those years as the best years four of a person's life long after I was done with college. If you are open to other people deciding for themselves which parts of their life are best, you can help them find what will truly make them happiest, whether or not it's the most common thing that society expects will make them happy.

## "Life Only Gets Harder!"

Finally, there is a more severe form of telling people that they are in the best time of their life, and that is saying, "If you think things are bad now, it's only going to get worse later on." This is a severe form of invalidation because, not only are you cutting down the person's problem by comparing it to future hypothetical problems and pushing them to accept things that are not okay, but when you say things like, "Life only gets harder," or "It will only get worse later on," you eliminate any hope that the person has of things getting better. If someone is having a horrible time, their only hope in the world might be that what they are going through will end at some point, that life will get better, and you are telling them that it will not. When I was having the worst time of my life in college and reached out for help, I was constantly being told that those years would be the best four years of my life and that everything would only get harder and worse afterwards. My classmates insisted to me that college was the easiest, least stressful time of my life and that things would only get harder after graduation. Even the counselors I spoke to on campus insisted that my college years were the best and that someday I would look back and realize that. I would have to be in an extremely terrible situation before I would ever wish to be back at college, and the counselors essentially told me that that's where I would be. My only hope was that my life could get better after college, but everyone kept tearing this hope away from me when they said that things would only get worse.

If you truly cannot relate to or empathize with someone who is in a different stage of life than you, just accept their feelings at face value, even if you never quite "get it." *Never eliminate someone's only hope of things getting better.*

When it comes to people's feelings, don't worry about the past or the future. Focus on what matters to the person right now.

## "Grow Up!"

Telling someone to "grow up" or "act your age" is a common form of invalidation. "Grow up!" normally implies that your feelings, behaviors, and reactions to things should be less than what they actually are, just because of your age. There's an assumption that the older you get, the less you will be upset when things don't go your way and the more you will be okay with doing things you don't want to do. This is not true of everyone. For instance, when you tell an older sibling to let their younger sibling have what they want just because they are younger, you don't know that the older sibling will actually be less upset about not getting what they want than the younger sibling, and it is not okay to force those standards on them. If someone is crying over something that you would not expect someone their age to cry about, *that is okay*. Their feelings are still valid, regardless of their age.

When I was in elementary school, our gym teacher always had us form teams randomly, such as by counting off every other person or using people's birth months. But for some reason, when we got to middle school, we started having captains who picked the players on their teams. The same people always got picked last, and it never felt good. There was no reason for us to begin picking teams in middle school when randomized teams had worked just fine throughout elementary school. (In fact, it was actually more efficient than having team captains). Picking teams caused a lot of hurt feelings that never existed back when we had random teams, and there was no reason for it – no reason other than that we were "old enough" to handle it. But the fact that we were older did not make us feel any less bad about being picked last.

Additionally, we should not assume that just because someone gets older, they will lose interest in or outgrow things that our culture associates with younger people. It's okay to enjoy the same things that you did when you were younger. I still played with my toys when I was a teenager. Most of my favorite books and movies are meant for kids. I still like building sandcastles and going sledding and playing tag and hide and seek, when I can find someone to play with. There are some expectations in our culture that people will outgrow things and "move on," but it is okay if that doesn't happen, for you or for anyone around you. It's okay to dress the way you want, listen to kind of music you like, and to do what makes you happy, regardless of your age.

# When the Shoes Don't Fit

For the most part, treating other people the way that we want to be treated is good advice. Stopping to put yourself in someone else's shoes and thinking, "How would I feel if this were happening to me? How would I want to be treated?" is a great way to be caring and considerate of people. But there are also times when our *need* to identify with others can actually prevent us from understanding their feelings. Take this example: Eliza gets angry very easily when people around her chew gum. She has tried asking people not to chew gum around her, but they don't take her seriously. Finally, one day, when a coworker is chewing gum right in Eliza's ear, Eliza yells at her coworker and storms out of the room. This story quickly becomes hot gossip, with everyone wondering what is wrong with Eliza.

In this case, everyone *did* imagine themselves in Eliza's position – they thought to themselves, "I wouldn't get so angry just because someone was chewing gum, so I don't understand why someone would react that way." But we have to understand that everyone is different, and that putting yourself in someone else's shoes doesn't mean that you will always feel the way they do about all of the same things. Focus on how the other person is *feeling*, not on the superficial details of what they were feeling that way about. Instead of thinking, "How does someone get so angry about gum-chewing?" think, "How would I feel if I were constantly subjected to something that caused a problem for me?" Even if there isn't any kind of noise that bothers you as much as the gum-chewing bothers Eliza, imagine how you'd feel if you had to endure *anything* that caused a problem for you for the entire day, such as getting poked with a sharp pencil or having ice cubes poured down your shirt. *That* may be what Eliza is experiencing when she has to be around gum-chewing. Eliza might have misophonia, a disorder which causes people to experience negative emotions upon hearing certain sounds. Treat Eliza with the respect, validation, and understanding that you would want to be treated with if something was constantly hurting you, even if gum-chewing in particular would not be a problem.

Here is another example: [Content: sexual assault] Your friend José says that he doesn't want to go to a certain club with you and your friends because the club always plays a song that he doesn't like. Your friends tell José to lighten up and they keep pressuring him to go to the club, insisting that everyone has songs they don't love and that shouldn't be a reason to miss out on a fun time. José gets very quiet and won't engage with anyone else. The rest of you head off to the club and some of your friends say that they don't understand what José's issue is. Later, when you talk to José alone, he reveals that he cannot listen to that song because it was playing while he was sexually assaulted, and hearing it now brings back traumatic memories for him. When his friends tried to convince him to go to the club, they were putting themselves in his position and saying, "If the club played a song that I don't like, that wouldn't be a reason to stay home!" But your friends don't share José's experience. Your friends may not have a song that triggers traumatic memories for them. They may not have a song that hurts them the way that this song hurts José. To be a good friend, they should listen to José and accept it when he says that he cannot go to the club that plays that song, even if they cannot identify with him.

### "But I'm Just Being a Good Friend!"

It's sometimes easy to tell when you are crossing someone's boundaries in order to get what *you* want. If you are borrowing someone's clothes without asking, or pressuring someone to join your club because you want more members, you probably understand that they don't appreciate it. But what happens when you're doing something that you think a friend *should* appreciate? Here is an example:

Courtney grew up in a family that loves to throw surprise parties. Anytime someone has a birthday, anniversary, or graduation and isn't planning their own celebration, Courtney and the rest of her family will surprise them with a party. They do this for all sorts of occasions – to congratulate people on their achievements, to cheer people up when they're feeling down, and just to remind people that they are loved. Courtney learned at a young age that throwing a surprise party is how you show a person that you care about them. She has given surprise parties to all of her friends, and so far, they have all appreciated it.

One day, Courtney throws a surprise party for her new friend, Noelle. She tells Noelle that just the two of them are getting some ice cream together, but as soon as they enter the ice cream shop, all of Noelle's friends jump out from under the booths and yell "SURPRISE!"

"Wow," says Noelle, taken aback. "Um…thank you…" She smiles politely, but doesn't seem as thrilled as Courtney's other friends

73

did when she threw surprise parties for them. Noelle is nice to everyone and seems to have a good time at the party, but after all the guests head home, Noelle pulls Courtney aside. "I appreciate you throwing this party for me," Noelle says. "It was really nice of you to think of me. But I'd prefer if in the future, you don't do this again. When you said we were getting ice cream just the two of us, that was what I wanted to do. I didn't like having this party sprung on me."

Courtney doesn't know how to react. She's gone her whole life with everyone appreciating her surprise parties and has never met anyone who didn't want them. Her first instinct is to criticize Noelle, to say something like, "You need to live a little!" or "Don't be wound up so tight!" or to make it her mission to get Noelle to like surprise parties.

When you're in a situation like this, try to remember that everyone likes different things, everyone has different boundaries, and it's okay if one person is not okay with something that other people would be okay with. Sometimes we grow up thinking that "everyone" responds well to a particular thing, and it can be difficult the first time we meet someone who doesn't like it. But keep in mind that just because you have never met someone who likes or doesn't like something does not mean that nobody like that exists. Even if you have never met someone like Noelle before, even if you're offended that she didn't like what you did for her, being a good friend means accepting that Noelle does not like surprise parties, agreeing not to throw her anymore surprise parties, and not pressuring her to learn to like them. Also, keep in mind that Noelle's reaction was a best-case scenario in which she stated her needs clearly and respectfully. In a different situation, Noelle might have exclaimed, "I hate surprise parties!" and stormed out, or she might not have said what was wrong but just looked miserable the entire time. Either of these things might make Courtney feel even more defensive, but they reflect the same situation, and it's better to accommodate your friends' needs even if they don't find the best way to express themselves. You can also learn from this experience with Noelle and be more accepting in the future by finding out if someone likes surprise parties before you throw them one.

# Subjective Reality

Think of a place that is at least an hour's drive away from where you are right now. Now imagine that a friend calls you from that place and says, "Meet me here in ten minutes!" You explain that it is impossible for you to get there that fast, but your friend just keeps insisting that it only takes ten minutes, and implies that there must be something wrong with you if it takes you an hour. How would you feel about that? Would this be a nice way for your friend to talk to you?

This is a way that we often communicate when we think we know how long something should take, or how easy something should be, without considering that it might be different for everyone. We assume that our own experience is the standard.

One time at my high school, a social studies class was taking a survey on how long students took to get ready for school in the morning. I said that it took me thirty minutes, and the two friends I was sitting with each said it took them ten minutes. My friends started asking what I did in the morning that took so long. They asked if I showered in the morning, and I said no, I did that at night. They asked if I ate a big breakfast, and I said no, I ate dry cereal on the way to school. I knew they were trying to figure out why I took longer than they did to get ready, but I just didn't want to engage with them because they were treating their experience as normal and my experience as weird. They were acting as if ten minutes was the standard amount of time that it should take a person to get ready, and that I needed a reason for taking longer. But for me, thirty minutes was normal, and I could have just as easily asked them if they cut time by sleeping in their clothes for the next day.

There is nothing wrong with having different experiences, but we should not treat some experiences as "normal" and others as "weird." If you and your friends are complaining about how much you hate a particular book series, and another friend joins you and says that they love this book series, don't just ignore this person and keep complaining about the series, and especially don't put down people who do like the series. If there is an awkward pause when your friend says that they love the series, let them know that it's okay. You could make a comment that it's fine for people to like different kinds of books. You can have a nice conversation about what you all like and don't like about the series, or you can just change the subject. If you suspect that everyone in the

75

group hates the series with a passion and your friend will be singled out, changing the subject is probably a better idea. It is better not continue on with the bashing session as if your friend is not there, or as if your friend's feelings do not matter. (That said, if someone holds an opinion that goes against your core values or violates human rights, you do not need to validate or accept it. This example only applies to situations where people have different preferences about things like food, music, or other things that don't harm anyone).

Accepting people's experiences is especially important when it comes to things that can make people feel better or worse about themselves, such as how difficult something is or how long it will take. If you just aced a test that you thought was easy, and a friend comes up to you complaining that the test was so hard and they think they failed, do not "correct" your friend and say, "What are you talking about? That test was easy!" This is likely to make your friend feel bad about themself. If you really need to tell someone that the test was easy for you, talk to someone who you know did as well as you did, or someone who is removed from the situation.

If you are with a group of friends who all agree that something was easy, be careful about not making people feel bad within that group. Before launching into a discussion about how easy the test was, make sure everyone in the group actually feels that way, and keep the conversation focused on the test itself. Avoid putting people down who didn't do well on the test or found it hard, even if there is no one like that sitting with you. Putting people down creates an unsafe environment. You may have all aced the test this time, but if anyone in the group finds the *next* test to be difficult, they will probably not feel safe talking to you if you have put people down in the past. Remind the group that the test was not necessarily easy for everyone, and maybe mention why it was easy for you. You could say that you had the right skills to do this exam easily, rather than simply saying that the test was easy.

If someone compliments you on something that you don't consider an accomplishment, be sensitive to their feelings in your response. When someone says, "Wow! You got an A on that paper? Great job!" that person might be revealing that they personally find papers hard and consider it a huge achievement to get an A. If you give the person a response that sounds like, "Why are you congratulating me for this?" you are telling the person that getting an A on a paper *should* be no big deal, when it might be something that they can only dream of achieving. Unless you find the compliment condescending – for example, if someone is being over-complimentary because they didn't expect you to do well – try to avoid putting the other person down for considering something an achievement. If you want to complain that you should have gotten a 100% on your paper instead of a 93%, talk to someone who would feel the same way or who is removed from the situation.

The amount of time a task will take is also a subjective measurement. If someone says that they have way too much homework, and then they tell you specifically what they have to do, don't correct them with, "That's not that much!" It *is* that much because the person already described it as "way too much" before they told you exactly what they had to do. It's their homework, and it's up to them to decide how much constitutes "too much." If someone says that they have so much reading to do that it will take them all week, and then they tell you the exact number of pages they have to read, try not to respond with, "That should only take a few hours!" It will *not* only take a few hours – your friend just told you that it would take them a week. "Correcting" your friend in this way is not only invalidating, but it is likely to make your friend feel bad about themself. There is nothing wrong with it taking your friend any length of time to do any amount of reading or work, and it is insulting to imply that something is wrong with them because it "should" take them less time. The world is full of standards of what everyone should be able to do and how long things should take. Your friend might already know that most people read faster than they do and they were trusting you to accept them. Your friend may have also been lucky enough to grow up *not* thinking that there is anything wrong with them, and you could be responsible for making them feel bad about something that they had never considered to be a problem before.

Sometimes, a person may take longer with a task because they have not learned the most efficient way to do it. If this is the case and you know a shortcut that would help someone go faster, then then by all means, share it. But otherwise, don't push your standards onto anyone else.

## "You'll Get Used to It"

People often assume that because I'm from a cold climate, I don't mind the cold. They often assume that because my cousin is from a warm climate, he doesn't mind the heat. In reality, I hate the cold and my cousin hates the heat. Being used to something does not make it okay. When someone is complaining about something new that they're experiencing, it is very common to tell them that they'll get used to it. This is sometimes true, but many times, a problem will not simply stop existing over time unless something is done to fix it.

There are certainly times when getting used to something will fix the problem, but that is only when the problem exists *because* something is new and different. For example, if you just moved to a new school and are upset because you have no one to talk to or sit with at lunch, this problem will hopefully fade over time once you start to know more people. If your friend is in a position like this, it might be helpful to assure them that this problem will fade over time, while also offering support for how they feel, and maybe some suggestions on how to make new friends.

Now, let's say that instead of simply not knowing anyone, you become a target for bullying as soon as you enter the school. You are facing constant stares, whispers, and insults every day. While this is a change from your old school, this not the kind of problem that will simply fade away over time. The harassment will not simply stop hurting once you get used to it going on every day. This is an example of a problem that needs to be dealt with.

There is a clear-cut distinction between the above examples. Most people can agree that it takes time to make friends at a new school, but that bullying is unacceptable. But there are many cases where it's not so obvious whether someone only needs time to adjust, or whether the situation will never become acceptable. Here are some examples of concerns that people might have about someone they know entering a new situation:

"She's a really picky eater."
"He's never been away from home before."
"They never do any physical activity."
"She hates crowds."
"He'll never go anyplace without cell phone service."
"They can't sit still for more than a few minutes."

These are the kinds of concerns where people often respond, "They'll get used to it." Now, it is definitely *possible* that these people might find that certain things are acceptable once they have tried them, but it is not guaranteed. Try to discuss these concerns the way you would discuss any other potential problem, rather than assuming that the issue will automatically go away.

I was once talking with some friends of my parents, when they told me that their daughter got a job as a counselor at an overnight summer camp. I was happy for their daughter, but I was also a bit surprised. From what I knew of their daughter, she liked a lot of quiet time to herself and was not outdoorsy. She didn't strike me as someone who would enjoy living at a camp all summer. I kept waiting for her parents to tell me how excited she was, but they never did. In our entire visit, her parents just kept reiterating that while their daughter was nervous, this would be a good experience for her. They said "good experience" in a tone that meant they thought it would be helpful to her, in terms of getting out of her comfort zone, but not once did they give any indication that she was actually looking forward to the job.

While I knew logically that she must have wanted the job since she applied for it, my stomach was in a knot during the conversation. In fact, I always cringe when I hear people saying that their children (or anyone they know) may not like something at first, but they'll get used to it. I cringe because for me, college was something that I was told I would "get used to," but the reality was that college life was not for me and I wanted to run back home just as badly at the end of my senior year as I did at the beginning of my first year. Time does not fix everything. If someone is thrown into a situation that is way out of their comfort zone, there is no guarantee that they will adjust and come out fine. I did not come out of college fine. If something is really not acceptable to someone, it will not just become acceptable after they've lived with it for a long time. And again, most of these things are not as obvious as the example of bullying.

No one likes being bullied, but many people are okay with activities like going away to college or being a counselor at an overnight camp. However, for some individuals, things that many people are okay with can be just as bad as the bullying.

Exercise: Think of three times that you were in a situation that was not acceptable for you, something that never would have become acceptable

79

no matter how long the situation lasted. If this has never happened to you, imagine something that you would hypothetically never become okay with:

1._____

2._____

3._____

Now, think of a time that another person was worried or uncertain about something, and you told them (or assumed) that they would get used to it. What could you have done differently to address their concerns? How could you have validated their feelings if the situation never became acceptable to them?

_____

_____

_____

## Don't Get Used to Someone Else's Problem

Imagine that your friend normally posts lots of happy things on social media, but they suddenly start complaining a lot after a change happens in their life. They get a lot of sympathy and support when the problem first begins, since this amount of complaining is not normal for them. But as time goes on and they continue to complain all the time, the support starts to fade. Everyone gets used to the fact that this person now complains all the time, and they don't think of what your friend is going through as a problem that needs to be addressed.

In reality, it does need to be addressed. Time does not fix everything, especially issues that are ongoing. If someone is complaining about something for months on end, that means that something is still wrong. Don't fall into the trap of getting used to your friends' problems to the point that you don't take them as seriously. If someone has been complaining about the same issue for months, that means it's a problem and it should be treated as such.

It is also important to note that the *lack* of complaining does not necessarily mean that everything is fine. If someone complained about something for a while, and then they gradually stopped complaining so much, this does not necessarily mean that the issue is resolved. Expressing yourself takes energy, and your friend could be so worn-down, either from the problem or from not being taken seriously, that they no longer have the energy to complain. In this situation, it can be helpful to ask your friend how they are feeling, rather than assuming that they must feel better.

## Some Words Speak Louder than Actions

Exercise: List five things you've done that you don't want to do again. These can be things you felt obligated to do, things you tried and found you didn't like, or things that you went along with in order to be polite or considerate of other people:

1._____
2._____
3._____
4._____
5._____

The purpose of this exercise is to remind you that even if you did something before, that does not mean that you want to do it again.

There is a spinoff of telling someone that they'll get used to something: Telling someone they should be okay with something just because they've done it before. We do things that we don't want to do all the time, and the fact that we did something once does not necessarily mean that we would be willing to do it again.

When my friend was signing the lease on her first apartment, the landlord warned her that the building could get loud on the weekends. My friend shrugged and said, "I've lived in a dorm." But what she really meant was, "I've lived in a dorm, and I know from that experience that I'm not bothered by noise." I had also lived in a dorm, and I knew from my experience that I would not want to live in a building that was loud on the weekends.

When someone tells us that they don't like something that they've done before, we often say, "But you looked like you were having fun!" The fact is, you are not always going to announce to everybody that you don't like something. Think about it: If you don't like your grandmother's mincemeat pie, would you announce that to the whole dinner table? If you're miserable on a day trip that everyone else loves, would you tell everyone that you hate the trip? Would you tell your brother that his wedding reception is boring and you want to go home?

When someone tells you that they don't like something, and you think to yourself, "But I *saw* you eating mincemeat pie," or "But you *looked* like you were having fun on the trip," take a step back, remember that we all have reasons for doing things we don't want to do, and believe what the person is telling you now. If your friend actually *wanted* to move to a noisy building or eat mincemeat pie or go on a trip, they would not be telling you that they don't.

# It's Not All-or-Nothing

While it is important to understand that some situations are just not acceptable for everyone, it is equally important to keep in mind that just quitting something entirely is not always the solution to the problem. I mentioned that I'm from a cold climate and I don't like the cold. During the winter, when everyone is complaining about the cold and the snow, there are always people who say, "If you don't like it, don't live here!" Every situation is not all-or-nothing. The fact that someone doesn't like the cold does not necessarily mean that they want to pack up and move someplace warmer. Moving is expensive and it is not something that everyone can afford to do. Even if someone can afford to move, moving is a major decision, and there could be plenty of other reasons that they want to stay where they are. The fact that someone does not want to move does not mean that they have to love everything about their situation and do not have the right to complain. While it's important to support someone in decisions such as moving, breaking up with a partner, finding a new job, or otherwise getting out of a situation that isn't working for them, it is also important to accept that quitting altogether is not always the solution that will work best for someone. Do not brush off people's complaints with, "If you don't like it, quit!" and imply that their only choices are to quit or stop complaining. People have the right to find fault with situations even when they do not want to get out of those situations altogether. If your friend is not looking to get out of a situation altogether, you can still validate their negative feelings about the situation. You can try help them feel better or resolve their issues, without pushing them to get out of the situation altogether.

## Don't Talk People Out of How They Feel

When someone tells you that they feel a certain way, do not use logic to try to talk them out of their feelings. Here are some examples:

Person 1: "I'm cold."

Person 2: "How can you be cold? It's hot in here and you're wearing a heavy sweater."

Person 1: "I'm hungry."

Person 2: "You just ate lunch."

Person 1: "I need to go to the bathroom."

Person 2: "You just went."

Even if the facts that Person 2 stated are all true, it does not make Person 1's feelings invalid. You *can* be cold when other people find it hot. You *can* still be hungry after lunch. You *can* have to go to the bathroom after you just went. Instead of trying to talk people out of how they feel, try to treat their feelings the same way that you would if they *did* make sense to you. Look for a bathroom. Offer someone a blanket. Grab a snack. If a child just ate and you think they might get too full if they eat right now, you could explain that it takes food a while to digest and that it might be better to wait fifteen minutes to see if they feel full.

If you don't think someone will like something, instead of *telling* them they shouldn't do it, try sharing the information that you have:

Instead of: "Don't go see that movie! It sucked!"

Try: "I didn't like that movie because I'm not into sci-fi movies, but I don't know how you'll feel about it."

Instead of: "You don't want to go to the concert!"

Try: "I heard that I concert is going to be really jam-packed, and you've mentioned that you don't like crowded places."

Instead of: "Don't take a class with Ms. Andersen!"

Try: "If you're thinking of taking a class with Ms. Andersen, just be aware that she assigns a lot of homework."

Instead of telling people what to do, try offering them information that will help them decide on their own.

## But They Just Want Attention!

Imagine that you're enjoying an afternoon in the park with your friends, when your friend Natasha steps aside to take a phone call. You hear a lot of screaming, and the next thing you know, Natasha comes running over and bursts into tears.

"What happened?" you ask her.

"I didn't get picked to be in my aunt's wedding!" she exclaims. "Both of my sisters get to be in the wedding but not me!" She drops to the ground and starts sobbing uncontrollably.

You go over to try to comfort her, but another friend pulls you aside and whispers, "She's just doing that for attention! Just ignore her!"

What should you do now?

First of all, it's hard to know what a person's true motivations are. If you ignore Natasha because you think she's just looking for attention, but she actually is just that upset, then that would be a huge betrayal. Remember, we shouldn't accuse people of "overreacting," because people react based on how much something matters to them. If someone has a bigger reaction to something than you would have expected, it could just mean that something is more important to them than it is to you. It could also be the tip of the iceberg of a bigger problem that you are not fully aware of. Blaming Natasha for wanting attention could just be a way to ignore the real issue.

Secondly, if Natasha *is* looking for attention, what would be the right thing for you to do? It probably wouldn't be to just ignore her. Attention is a basic human need. So, when someone is crying for attention, that shows an unmet need. If Natasha has been ignored or mistreated in the past, she may feel the need to be louder or more dramatic to make sure that anyone listens to her at all. Think about it – if you're trapped in a ten-foot hole and scream for help but no one hears you, you're going to scream louder until someone does hear you. So, if you just ignore Natasha now, it will likely escalate the situation by making her feel even more desperate.

In this case, all Natasha probably needs is for you to stay with her while she is crying and to listen and validate her feelings. Now, validating someone's feelings does not necessarily mean that you will meet *all* of their emotional needs. You can be supportive of Natasha, even if you don't want to get involved in her family conflict. If Natasha ends up asking for more support than you are willing to provide, you can be clear with her about what your limits are – that way, she will know that you are taking her seriously, even if you can't give everything that she wants. Ultimately, you can validate and support Natasha the same way that you would if you were not questioning whether she might just be looking for attention.

## But Everyone Feels That Way!

Sometimes, when a friend is complaining about a problem, we brush their feelings off with, "But everyone feels that way!" We indicate that if everyone else feels just as bad and isn't complaining, then this person should not be complaining either. This can be invalidating for many reasons:

1.     First of all, you don't know for sure if everyone else actually feels the same way. Maybe "everyone" feels lonely when they first arrive in a new place, for example, but you don't know that every single person who says they are lonely feels as bad as your friend does. There are different levels of every emotion, and just because other people say, "I'm nervous," "I'm disappointed," "I'm lonely," etc. does not mean that they are all experiencing the same levels of these emotions. Some people might be experiencing these emotions to a much greater degree than others.

2.     Secondly, even if other people were experiencing the exact same feelings as your friend, it wouldn't matter. Your friend can react however they want to react. If other people choose not to talk about their problems, that is their personal choice, just as it may be your friend's personal choice to tell their problems to everyone they meet or post them all over social media. Also, the fact that other people are not complaining is not morally better. Even if someone isn't complaining, that does not necessarily mean that they are against complaining – they might *want* to complain but be afraid that no one will listen to them, or they could feel that they have to pretend to be happy and positive in order to keep their friends. This can especially be true if they have had their feelings invalidated in the past. It is perfectly fine if you don't feel like sharing your feelings, but you shouldn't act like that's a better way to be.

3.     Third, everyone has different abilities.   Imagine that two members of a bowling league each break their dominant arm. One of them has always been well-coordinated on both sides and is able to quickly learn how to play well with their non-dominant arm. The other person was never very coordinated on their non-dominant side, and never manages to get up to speed.  The injury is the same, but these people had different abilities that related to how well they could function in spite of the injury. This does not make the person who "bounced

back" any better than the person who didn't – it just means that they had certain skills.

Now, imagine a different scenario in which the bowlers have equal levels of coordination, but the resources that they can spend on adapting to their arm being broken are very different. Maybe one person is a single parent who works two jobs, and bowling once a week is the only time they have for themself, whereas the other person has a lot of free time to practice bowling. Maybe one person is mentally bogged down with school, work, or family obligations, while the other person comes to bowling practice rested and refreshed, and has an easy time concentrating. Maybe one person can afford to pay for physical therapy and the other can't.

The same is true for emotional needs. Some people are compartmentalizers, and their work performance and behavior will not be affected as much by other things. Some people are not compartmentalizers, and everything that they do will be deeply affected by what is wrong. We should respect both kinds of people. When it comes to resources, some people may have a huge support system that meets all of their emotional needs, and some people might not. Some people get as much paid leave as they need when something goes wrong, and some people aren't given the recovery time that they need.

4.      People have different priorities. You may want something so badly that it comes first on your list – above getting enough sleep, spending time with family and friends, having fun, relaxing, and just having a pleasant life. That's fine, but everyone does not have those priorities. You may want something so badly that you will try your hardest to push through even when you're really miserable, but that does not mean that every person in your position will want to do that. If your friend is having a hard time at college and you tell them that "everyone" else at your college misses home as well, but they are still able to function and succeed, the people you are referring to may have decided that succeeding in college was their highest priority and that they would try their best to push through even if they aren't happy. Someone else may place their emotional needs and the pleasantness of their experience as a higher priority and not be willing to push through when their most important needs are not met, which is also okay.

5.      Finally, and most importantly, *"normal" does not mean "okay."* The fact that everyone goes through a difficult time does not make it

any less bad for any of those individual people. The counselors I spoke to in my first year of college told me that what I was going through was "normal," but they said "normal" as if it meant "okay." They essentially told me, "Don't worry, you're fine," when I was trying to communicate that I was *not* fine. A problem does not have to be uncommon for it to be a legitimate problem. Lots of horrible things are common experiences, but that does not make any of those things acceptable.

If a person feels isolated, like they are the only one who is going through what they are going through, it can be helpful to show them that other people are experiencing the same thing. However, if you go this route, your goal should be to help *connect* your friend to other people they can relate to, perhaps by recommending a club, support group, online forum, blog, or community where they can connect with other people who have similar issues. Telling someone that other people are going through the same thing should only be an attempt to help them find support and to feel less alone, not a way of dismissing their problem. "Normal" and "common" do not equal acceptable.

## Types of Pain

There are different types of physical pain. First, there's the kind of pain that you don't want to experience, like burning your hand on a hot stove or spraining your ankle. But there's another kind of pain that can actually feel good, such as the pain you might feel during an intense workout, or from stretching your muscles when they've been stiff. This can vary from person to person – someone who loves running might be perfectly fine pushing through muscle pain in order to win a race, whereas someone who does not enjoy running might prefer not to experience that pain at all.

When it comes to mental and emotional stress, the same is true – there are kinds of stress that you just don't want to experience (even if you are stuck with those types of stress), and there are kinds of stress that you do want to experience, or that you are willing to work through for the benefits. Whether a particular stressor is okay or not okay will vary from person to person as well.

Imagine that you and your friend are both entering a new situation together, for instance, starting a new job. To you, starting this new job is a fun, exhilarating experience that you're looking forward to. It reminds you of something that gives you the jitters in a good way, such as performing in a talent show or playing a sports game. But to your friend, starting this new job is something that they are absolutely dreading. To them, it's on the level of getting a tooth pulled. If your friend tries to comfort you in the way that they would like to be comforted, it might cause you to worry about things that you were actually excited about. If you try to encourage your friend the way that you would like to be encouraged, you might end up invalidating your friend's feelings and pressuring them to be positive about something that just isn't positive for them. To fix this problem, it would help for you and your friend to acknowledge that this is a different experience for each of you. Let your friend know that you are psyched about this new opportunity, but also let them know that you accept the fact that they are not looking forward to starting a new job and that you are not going to try to pressure them to like the experience.

Exercise: List some examples of stressors that you do not like to experience at all (even if you do experience them a lot):

_____

_____

_____

_____

Now list some examples of things that are stressful but give you a positive feeling at the same time, or that you are willing to go through for the positive outcome:

_____

_____

_____

_____

Review these lists with your friends so that you can learn more about each other, and about the different kinds of support that you need in different situations. The support that you want when you fall down and break your leg is probably different from the support you want when you are training for a race that you're both nervous and excited about. When it comes to stressful things, talk about when you'd like to be encouraged and cheered on, and when you'd like support because you are going through something that is difficult for you. Don't automatically encourage your friends to push through pain and think about the positive side of everything they do. Everyone is different, and it is perfectly okay if someone does not want certain stressors in their life at all, even if you feel good about the same experiences.

# Legitimate Reasons

One of the most important parts of validating people is accepting what they say as legitimate. This means that if someone gives an excuse or reason that they were unable to do something – even a reason that seems strange to you – you do not question whether or not their excuse is "good enough." Validating people means believing them at face value and accepting that if they said that they were unable to do something, they were unable to do it. It is not up to you to determine whether or not their reason is legitimate. Only they can make that call.

That said, this does not mean that you need to give other people everything that they want or accept everything that they do. Your feelings are valid as well, and if you feel that it was unfair for someone to break their commitment, or that they are not doing their share of the work, it is fine to say so. You just want to keep the focus on the problem at hand, and not on whether or not their reasons are "legitimate." Try looking for ways to resolve the problem by accommodating the person's needs so that they can do what they need to do. If someone has a problem with a situation – for example, they don't want to go to meetings because the room has fluorescent lights or because someone is wearing a heavy perfume that makes them feel sick – these issues can be accommodated. If someone missed an important meeting because they weren't feeling well enough to go, or if they didn't give a clear reason, don't focus on whether or not you think their reason was "legitimate" enough for them to miss the meeting. Talk about how *you* feel about them missing the meeting and what you feel the problem is. Some examples of what to say:

1. "I understand that you couldn't make it to the meeting yesterday, but it feels like Tonia and I are doing most of the work on this project." Give them a chance to offer to do something. If they don't offer, you could suggest a way that they can contribute.

2. "I was upset that you had to cancel plans at the last minute. We picked this date because everyone could make it and I had my entire week organized around this meeting." Give them a chance to apologize, and discuss what can be done to prevent this problem going forward, such as calling each other when you have to cancel rather than just not showing up.

I once did a project in a group of four people, in which three of us worked hard on the project, and one student did almost no work.

93

We'll call that one student Alison. At the time, it annoyed me that Alison didn't do her share of the project, but looking back on it now, there are a number of reasons why she may not have participated. First of all, she may not have understood the project. We never discussed the logistics of the assignment – the other three of us just dove right in, with the expectation that we all knew what we were doing. If we had asked whether everyone understood what to do, we might have been able to help Alison so that she could do her share. It's also possible that Alison was just less assertive and not as comfortable talking in groups as the rest of us were. With the three of us confidently voicing all of our ideas, perhaps Alison felt intimidated and just wasn't the type to push herself into the middle of such an assertive group. We could have been more sensitive to that by giving everyone a turn to share, rather than all jumping in at once. We could have specifically asked Alison for her input when she wasn't offering it on her own. Alternatively, Alison might have had something serious going on – a physical or mental health issue, or a traumatic life event – that was affecting her ability to work on the project, and she didn't feel comfortable telling us. When you are in an environment where everyone expects you to perform at a certain level, it can be hard to tell people that you have a problem because you never know whether they will accept it. We should have asked Alison if everything was okay, as her lack of involvement could have been a sign of a problem. Finally, we did a lot of communication on the project through email, but we never asked whether everyone had Internet access at home. (This was before smartphones were common). It's possible that Alison got left out because she simply couldn't respond to emails and add to shared documents as easily as the rest of us could. When everyone assumes that everyone has something like Internet access, it can be difficult to tell the group that you don't. We should have made sure that everyone could access their email easily before assuming that email was a good way to communicate. I know it's possible that Alison just didn't want to do any of the work, but it's also possible that Alison needed help or accommodations that the rest of us weren't giving her. If we had figured out a way to do the project that worked for all of us, Alison might have done her share and been a great project partner to work with.

# But No One Else Feels That Way!

Imagine that you've just gotten back from the worst weekend trip of your life, whatever that might be for you. Maybe you spent the whole time walking around in extreme heat or cold without the proper clothing. Maybe your friends spent all their time shopping in designer stores that you can't afford. Maybe the trip was centered around bungee jumping when everyone knows you're afraid of heights. Whatever the reason, it's not something you'd want to endure again. But all your friends absolutely loved the trip and want to go back again next weekend. When you say no thanks, the trip wasn't for you, everyone is in the state of shock. Some people even act offended, like they can't believe you would say something bad about such a wonderful weekend. When you try to explain that you didn't like the first trip, everyone keeps insisting that the trip was objectively awesome and that there must be something wrong with *you* if you didn't like it.

What you've just experienced is being an outlier, someone who deviates from the norm. We are often quick to invalidate outliers. If a school, workplace, or community is known for being friendly and welcoming, and we meet someone who hates the place, we often decide that the person must just have a bad attitude since no one else is complaining. If a person is popular among almost everyone, and we meet someone who can't stand them, we may automatically assume that the person who dislikes the popular person must be the source of the problem.

I once had a job interview where the hiring manager emphasized that everyone loved the company and that there was an almost zero turnover rate. The workplace culture seemed friendly and supportive, and I was hoping to get the job. On my second interview, after the manager reiterated to me that everyone was happy and loved it there, he shared that the last person who had left the company – the person who previously held the position I was applying for – hated the company and didn't get along with anyone, but that was because "she had issues." Now, I don't have a problem with someone not liking the company and leaving. That's normal. That's something that I would expect to happen at even the nicest companies because everyone just isn't suited for every type of job and workplace environment, and some people just don't click with each other. But after the manager spent a good portion of my interview complaining about his past employee and her "issues," I couldn't help feeling uneasy. He portrayed this former employee as someone who was just angry at the world and would never be happy anywhere. He tried to convince me that whatever happened was all this employee's fault and that no one else at the company did anything to cause a conflict for her. I understand that a high turnover rate is a bad sign, but having a manager who was not even open to possibility that the company may not be a good fit for everyone was also cause for concern.

There's a common fallacy that if someone has a conflict with everyone, it must be their own problem. When applying for jobs, most of us are taught to never mention conflicts with other people as a reason for leaving past workplaces, because no matter what the other people did or how unaccepting the community is, saying you had a conflict with anyone is going to make it look like you *are* the problem. Having conflicts with lots of people does not necessarily mean that you are the one causing the problem. If you are being bullied by a group of people, *they* are the ones doing something wrong. You are not responsible for their actions towards you. The same is true for anyone who has had a conflict with a large group of people. Groups of people – entire communities – can be unwelcoming to certain people. When you're accepted by your community, it's hard to see ways in which it might not be accepting to other people:

- If you are white, you might not see that your community is unwelcoming to people of color, that people regularly make racist comments, or that they treat certain people as outsiders because of their race.
- If you are cisgender, you might not see that your community is unwelcoming to transgender people. Your community might not use people's correct names and pronouns, they might insist that people dress in gender-conforming ways, and they might not allow people to use the bathroom that is right for them.
- If you are straight, you might not notice that your community is unwelcoming to gay, lesbian, or bisexual people. Your community might assume that everyone is straight, make anti-gay jokes, or refuse to give same-sex partners the same benefits they give to opposite-sex partners.

- If you are able to do your schoolwork or your job exactly as you are expected to do it, you may not be aware of the lack of accommodations available for people who have disabilities that you don't have.
- If you have plenty of money to spend on fun activities, you may not stop to think about how someone with less money might not be included when your group does something expensive.
- If you and your friends love to talk about diets and exercise, you may not realize how much of a problem this could be for someone who struggles with an eating disorder.

When someone has a long list of people who have hurt them or places that didn't accept them, it's easy to invalidate their experience by placing the blame on them, because they are the common denominator across all of the situations. But being the common denominator does *not* mean that someone will just never be happy in any situation. The person could have traits that other people do not usually accept or accommodate. Any environment can be unwelcoming to someone, and that does not mean that anything is wrong with the individual.

Exercise: Think of three people you know well. Now, think of a situation for each of these people that would be a living nightmare for them, but would not necessarily be a problem for everyone:

1. Person:_____
Situation:_____

_____

2. Person:_____
Situation:_____

_____

3. Person:_____
Situation:_____

_____

The purpose of this exercise is to help you understand that what is a nightmare for one person might be perfectly fine for someone else. That fact that all nightmare situations are not universal does not make them any less real.

## Personal Bias

I have a best friend who does not experience love as an emotion and does not have emotional attachments to other people. When my friend first shared this information with me, I was in disbelief. I had

97

always thought that love was universal. I didn't think it was possible to not experience love and still be happy. I had grown up believing that anyone who didn't love must be evil. But my friend is perfectly happy not experiencing love, and my friend still likes to help other people, it's just more because of a belief in social justice than because of emotional attachments. When my friend told me about how their mind worked, it was difficult for me to process, because it contradicted everything that I already believed. My friend has had lots of people deny their experience because it goes against what most people believe is true of everyone. Sometimes it takes a conscious effort to accept people's experiences at face value, and to allow the new information to change our previously held beliefs.

It's easy to invalidate people's experiences that are very different from our own. If someone says that they developed depression as a result of spending the summer with their grandparents, and you have long believed that spending time with your grandparents is always a positive experience because you have a great relationship with *your* grandparents, you might automatically reject your friend's story. You might make a comment like, "You're overreacting!" or, "You're just focusing on the negative," or "Spending time with your grandparents is awesome! You must not be making the best of it." Even if you don't say any of these comments out loud, you may be *thinking* that your friend is wrong about their own experience, which will affect how you treat them. It's important to validate your friend's experience even when it seems strange to you. You can even consciously say to yourself later, "Wow, I thought that *everyone's* grandparents treated them well, but I guess I was wrong." Sometimes we have to make a conscious effort to believe people about their experiences, but in doing this, we not only validate the person we are talking to, but we become more accepting and more able to validate other people's feelings in the future.

## Systematic Oppression

[Content: Examples of various forms of bigotry and discrimination]

It's easy to assume that everyone experiences the world the same way that you do, but such assumptions are often wrong. Maybe your teachers automatically see you as a good student and tend to give you the benefit of the doubt, while they automatically see some of your peers as troublemakers because of their race. Maybe you take it for granted that you can introduce your opposite-sex partner to anyone you want, while some of your friends have to be cautious who they introduce their same-sex partner to. Maybe you've always assumed that you would be judged based on your skills when you apply for a job, while someone of your peers know that they will be judged more harshly because of their race, sex, or gender identity. Maybe you take for granted that you can go wherever you want to go, while your peers who have mobility disabilities cannot access all of the same places. Maybe most tasks that you need to do every day are manageable for you, whereas some of your peers are just not able to do what your culture requires you to do in order to be successful. If a friend tells you that they are being treated unfairly, or that something is a problem for them when it is not a problem for you, try not to shut them down and tell them that everyone is treated the same, or that they just need to try harder. Remember that everyone does not have the same experience of the world, and understand that you may not see the ways in which your friend is treated differently than you are. Listen and learn about your friend's experience.

When someone experiences a form of oppression that you do not, accept that their experience is every bit as real as yours, even if it is very different from yours. Avoid trying to convince someone that the oppressions they face do not exist, or are not unique to people of their social group.

Here is an example: Monique and Holly are good friends. Monique is Black and Holly is white. One day when they are talking, Monique tells Holly about the harassment that she experienced as a child and the racial slurs that other kids used to call her. She talks about how her teachers often assumed that she would be trouble and were harsher on her than on her white classmates, and how a teacher even accused her of cheating because he didn't believe that she could have done so well. Holly responds by saying, "I know what you mean! I used to get bullied in school too and I had some teachers who hated me. I know exactly how you feel!"

At first glance, it may look like Holly is empathizing with Monique. She is saying, "Yes, I agree that everything you said is valid – I've experienced the same thing myself." The problem here is that Holly has not had the experience Monique is describing. All of the experiences that Monique has described are directly related to racial inequality. Holly does not have this experience. This does not mean that Holly's experiences of being mistreated are invalid, but for Holly to share her experience in this particular context puts the focus back on herself and interferes with what Monique was trying to say. It says, "Everyone gets treated badly sometimes, this is not specifically related to race," when Monique is trying to explain that everything is *not* equal and that she is affected by racism in a way that Holly is not. It is great to find common ground with other people, but when someone is talking about an issue related to their identity, such as race, sex, sexual orientation, gender identity, or socioeconomic status, you should not tell the person that you have the same experience as them when you do not share that identity.

Also, keep in mind that even if you do share a certain identity with someone, they could still face oppressions that you do not because of other factors. For example, if you and your friend are both bisexual, you could have different experiences with oppression. Being bisexual could be more acceptable in your religion and your culture than it is in your friend's religion and their culture. If you and your friend have different jobs and different interests, your friend may be part of communities that do not accept them in the way that your communities accept you. Your friend may not have the support system that you have with your friends and family. While it's wonderful to be able to connect over shared experiences, be open to learning about oppressions people experience that are different from yours.

You do not need to share someone's experience to accept that it is real. Listen, and learn how you can be supportive. It's okay to admit to your friend that you don't fully understand what they are going through. In addition to listening to your friend, do some research about the kind of discrimination your friend faces and how you can be a better friend to them. There are many resources online that will help you. While it's great to ask questions and learn from your friend, keep in mind that they may already be tired of explaining their issues to people, and they are not obligated to do the work of educating you if they don't want to.

## Respect People's Feelings about Their Identities

Here are some ways that you can respect the way people identify themselves and the way that they feel about their identities:

1.　　Believe people about their own experiences. If one person tells you that other people discriminated against them, and another person says, "No, we didn't," believe the person who experienced the discrimination, because only they know what they experienced. If someone punches you and it hurts, the fact that the person claims they didn't hit you very hard does not minimize your pain. When someone tells you that they were hurt by an action, that pain is completely real even if the other person says that they didn't do anything that "should" have been offensive.

2.　　Respect the fact that everyone does not consider every trait to be a major part of who they are. Do not just *expect* everyone who shares a particular identity to join clubs or activist communities relating to that identity, or discuss any issues in detail with you.

3.　　Only refer to a difference as a disability if the person calls it a disability themself. Be aware that some people may consider a difference to be a disability, while other people refer to the same difference as an advantage, or as a neutral trait. Accept however a person identifies.

4.　　Don't try to convince someone that something is positive when they consider it a disadvantage, such as by telling someone who has a physical disability that they are lucky they don't have to take gym class, or by telling someone with a learning disability that they are lucky to get extra time on tests. People may not feel lucky about these things themselves, so let them make that call.

5.　　Don't call someone "inspirational" just for living their life, unless you know that the person likes being described this way. If someone has written a book or given motivational talks about how they have triumphed over adversity, or if they regularly talk about their story in a way that tries to be inspirational, then by all means, let the person know that they have inspired you. But if someone does not refer to themself as an inspiration, don't try to make them into one. Referring to someone as "inspirational" for doing things that most people do makes it sound like you have lower expectations of their abilities, and can make a person feel alienated.

6.     Accept that you cannot tell everything about a person just by looking at them, and be open to learning things about people that you never would have suspected. Think of some qualities about yourself and your life experiences that people can't guess just by looking at you – the fact that you love peanut butter and raspberry sandwiches, that you have two dogs, three cats, and a guinea pig, that your life dream is to be a rap singer. Now, imagine that when you share a piece of information about yourself, another person's reaction is, "That can't be true! You seem like a normal person! You're just using that as an excuse so you'll get special treatment!" This may sound silly, but this is actually a common reaction when someone who appears "normal" tells you that they have an issue that you were not aware of. If someone shares something personal with you, *believe them.* You are not doing someone a favor by saying that they don't seem "like that" – you are denying their experience.

7. If someone tells you that they have a physical or mental illness or disability:

Don't:

- Say, "But you seem normal!"

- Accuse the person of making it up so that they can have special treatment.

- Say that a person doesn't "look" like they are in as much pain as they are describing. The fact that someone has not outwardly expressed their pain does not mean that it does not exist. People will not always outwardly express their pain.

- Say that they don't have enough bad things in their life to have the issue that they have. Don't ask questions like, "What do you have to be depressed about?"

- Minimize their struggle by saying things like "everyone gets nervous sometimes" to someone who has an anxiety disorder, or "I'm so OCD too!" to someone who actually has OCD, when you don't.

- Act as if the person is choosing to have an illness or disorder and can choose to "snap out of it."

Do:

- Listen and accept what the person says.

- Validate them by saying something like, "Wow, that sounds really hard."
- Accept that the person cannot control their illness or disability. Accept that it is not their choice.
- Ask if there is anything you can do to better accommodate them.
- Educate yourself on your friend's condition to better understand it.
- Ask if what they have shared with you is private before you mention it to anyone else.

Think of a task that you cannot do: balancing on a tightrope, lifting three hundred pounds, etc. Now, imagine that you live in a culture where you are expected to do this task in order to function in society, that almost every school, workplace, and social group is designed with the assumption that you can do it. This is a reality for a lot of people. Keep this in mind when you meet someone who struggles with something that you assume is no big deal.

If someone tells you that they would have difficulty with a particular task, listen and work with them to find a solution. For example, if your project partner cannot read a book about child abuse because it triggers their PTSD, you can work together to find a different book that will be okay for both of you. If your partner has a migraine and cannot meet you, you can work out a different time to meet. If you know that someone in your group has an issue that may cause them to miss meetings and deadlines, you can discuss the issue and plan ahead. You could have people email their work to the group if they can't make a meeting at the last minute.

Being fair to everyone does not always mean dividing tasks evenly, because some tasks that are non-issues for one person may be incredibly difficult, painful, or traumatic for another person. If one person has a lot of anxiety about making phone calls, but another person can make phone calls without a problem, it makes sense for the person who does not have anxiety to make the phone calls, while the other person does a different task. If a particular task will hurt someone or cause more problems for them than it would for other people, listen and find a way to divide the tasks that works best for everyone.

Exercise: List any differences that you would like other people to accommodate, and how you would like them to accommodate you:

1. Difference:_____

How to accommodate:

_____

_____

2. Difference:_____

How to accommodate:

_____

_____

3.Difference:_____

How to accommodate:

_____

_____

Go over this exercise with your friends so that you can all learn how each other would like to be treated. Feel free to add more than three differences.

[Content: reference to abuse and sexual assault] Just as validation means believing people about any differences they may have, it also means believing people about events in their life. Imagine that someone you love passed away, and when you told your friends about it, expecting them to offer their condolences, they said things like, "Your grandfather couldn't have died!" "He was healthy and wouldn't do something like that!" "Are you *really* sure that's what happened?" "You're overreacting. He's probably just taking a nap!" How would you feel? It would seem ridiculous for anyone to say those things, but unfortunately, statements like this are common when someone says that they have been abused, raped, or sexually assaulted. If someone tells you that they were raped or abused, *believe them.* There is no reason to tell someone that they are lying, and most people don't lie about things like this. The odds are that you do know lots of people who were abused or raped and just have not shared that information with you. It is easy to say, "I don't think [the abuser] would have done that, so you must be lying." It is not a question of whether someone *would* have done something – they *did* do it. Again, rape and abuse are common, so it is likely that you do know someone who has done these things to someone. Always believe people about these experiences.

Don't Validate Someone by Invalidating Someone Else

When someone makes a statement against a group of people, be sure to validate *everyone* involved. Don't invalidate some people in order to validate others. Here are some examples:

1.     Someone says that they prefer to hire men because they think that men are logical, rational thinkers and women are too emotional. This is clearly not okay, but there is more than one problem going on here. One issue is that it's incredibly sexist to assume that all women are more emotional and less logical just because they are women. The second issue is that this statement implies that being emotional is an undesirable trait. This statement discriminates not only against women who don't fit the description, but against women who *are* very emotional and are also perfectly qualified for the job. This statement also pressures women who are emotional to pretend that they are not in order to be taken seriously. When you *only* argue against a sexist statement with, "Not all women are like that," you leave out the point that there is nothing wrong with being emotional, and that it's a problem that some traits are valued higher than others because of people's incorrect assumptions about what genders they go with.

2.     You and your friends are walking through a grocery store when you see a woman with a shopping cart overflowing with candy, soda, and chips. Your friends whisper some rude comments about her, and you say to them, "Hey, you don't know that she's gonna eat all of that herself. Maybe she's having a party!" While you are doing the right thing by standing up for this woman, your reasoning indicates that it *would* be acceptable to make rude comments if she *were* going to eat all the food herself. That in itself is not respecting this woman and her choices. She is a human being and deserves to be treated with respect regardless of what she is eating.

3.     It is holiday season and everyone around you has been in good spirits, except for one friend who has been moping around all month. You've been trying to get him to cheer up and have fun like everyone else, but he won't change his mood. When he finally shares with you that this is a difficult time of year for him because it is the anniversary of his mother's death, you say, "Oh. *Now* I understand!" When you respond this way, you show that you are only respectful of his feelings now that you know the reason, while maintaining the idea that it would

not have been okay if he simply weren't in a cheerful mood during the holidays.

4.     Some classmates are teasing your friend, saying that he is gay because of how he dresses and acts. You stand up for your friend by asserting that he is definitely not gay. While it's great to step in and help your friend, telling people to leave him alone because he is straight implies that it *would* be okay to be mean to him if he were gay. It is important to call out your classmates for using "gay" as an insult in the first place.

5.     Your friend asks, "Do I look fat in these pants?" and you answer, "No, you look great!" This implies that you would think it was bad if your friend did look fat.

6.     When writing an advertisement about how much fun a summer camp or college community is, you say, "If you're not having fun here, it's your own fault. There is always lots to do!" This denies the experiences of people who are just not suited for that specific program, or who would not receive the accommodations that they need to participate in the activities that they would enjoy. You do not need to put people down in order to emphasize how much fun the place is.

8.     You label low-fat or sugar-free foods as "guilt-free," implying that someone was supposed to feel guilty about what they eat in the first place.

9.     You say that you deserve respect, privacy, freedom to make your own choices, etc. because you are an adult. This indicates that children do not have a right to these things, and that children's needs and desires are less valid than yours.

10.     You tell someone that they are really pretty or smart *for someone like them.* You say something like, "You're really pretty for a Black girl!" and expect it to be taken as a compliment, when you are actually implying that Black girls are not normally pretty. Upon learning that someone is lesbian, you say, "But you're so pretty!" Upon learning that someone has ADHD, you say, "But you're so smart!" You say in a surprised tone, "Wow, you're very articulate!" to a person of color, implying that you did not expect someone of their race to be articulate. Or you tell someone that you don't notice a particular quality about them: "I don't think of you as Black," "You're not like other Asian girls," "You don't act autistic." "Complimenting" someone by telling

them that you can't tell that they are what they are is *not* a compliment. It implies that you think there is something wrong with what they are.

An important part of validation is that respect is a basic human right. Respect should never need to be justified. It should never come in the form of, "We should respect this person because they don't *really* possess those qualities that other people like them possess." *Everyone* deserves respect. When people are putting someone down for a particular quality, don't try to deny that quality or claim that the person doesn't actually have that quality – make it clear that having that quality is *perfectly okay*, and that the person deserves to be treated with respect no matter what.

### "But I'm Not Like That!"

Think of a time when someone told you that you did something hurtful to someone – either directly to them or to a group of people – and you felt defensive. You immediately thought, "That's not me! I'm not racist. I'm not sexist. I'm not a bully. I just wouldn't do something like that!" Maybe you even started racking your brain for information that would prove that you are not the kind of person who does what you did. If, for example, you dress as a Native American for Halloween and someone points out that it is racist to use someone's culture as a costume, you may try to rationalize why your costume is not problematic because you don't want to think of yourself as being racist. You may tell yourself that there was nothing wrong with your costume because you didn't mean it be offensive, and that the other person is just being overly sensitive. And if you do brush off other people as "overreacting," you will have a much easier time continuing to brush off incidents like this in the future. But this isn't the right way to approach the situation. Instead of trying to defend yourself as not being racist, it would be better to admit that you did something wrong, apologize sincerely, and work on not making the same mistake going forward.

You may have an easier time handling situations like this if you avoid building your identity around the way you treat others. If you consider yourself "accepting," for example, think of accepting other people as an *action*, rather than a quality that you possess. And use "try" statements. Instead of saying, "I'm always accepting of people from all cultural backgrounds," say, "I try to be accepting of people from all cultural backgrounds." Instead of saying, "I'm always sensitive to other people's needs," say, "I try to be sensitive to other people's needs." When you think of a quality as being a part of who you are, it can feel like a personal attack on your character when someone tells you that you messed up. Your identity may feel threatened – you may feel like if you admit that you were inconsiderate to someone who is different from you, you can no longer call yourself an accepting person. This threat to your character can cause you to invalidate other people's feelings. But if you identify as someone who *tries* to be accepting of everyone, *tries* to be sensitive to people's needs, or *tries* to be an ally to people who experience forms of oppressions that you don't, then there is still room for you to make mistakes, apologize, and learn from them.

# Be Like the Sun

Sometimes it gets annoying when someone acts defensive about everything, when they seem guarded around you and always prepared to argue or fight, even though you think you are being a good friend to them. The fact is, people can become defensive from being invalidated, pressured, hurt, and betrayed throughout their lives. Think about it: if someone breaks into your home and steals from you, you're probably going to feel violated and will most likely become more on-guard. You may not want to leave your valuables unattended at work, even if that's what everyone else is doing. You may become cautious about not letting anyone know when you aren't home, and ask friends not to tag you in social media posts that reveal your whereabouts. You may have a hard time trusting people, and be very on-guard, and it would only make you feel worse for your friends to tell you that you're being silly and that you have nothing to worry about.

The same feeling of being on-guard can come from emotional pain. If you have something about you that most people don't accept, or that you have been attacked for in the past, it can be difficult to trust *anybody*. People don't walk around with signs on their foreheads naming the secrets they can be trusted with and the qualities that they will accept about a person. You might be thinking to yourself, "Why doesn't this person trust me? I'm safe," but the fact is, there may have been other people who looked exactly like you, yet still violated that person's trust. If those other people appeared "safe" – safe to talk to about specific issues, safe to trust with deep emotions, safe to physically be alone with, etc. – then how would that person know that you are any different? When someone is defensive or doesn't trust you, they may have been hurt in the past. Don't push someone to trust you when they don't. You can learn about their issues, and gradually work to earn their trust.

There is an Aesop's fable called "The Wind and the Sun," in which the wind and the sun are arguing about which of them is more powerful. They see a traveler approaching down the road, and the wind says, "Okay, let's settle this argument once and for all. Whichever one of us can make that traveler take off his coat is more powerful." The sun agrees. As the traveler approaches, the wind blows as hard as it can, trying to blow off the man's coat. But the harder the wind blows, the tighter the man grips onto his coat. The wind blows and blows and the

109

man clings tighter and tighter to his coat, until the wind has no more air left. Then the sun shines down on the traveler, making it warm and comfortable outside. The traveler starts to get warm, decides that it is such a nice day that he doesn't need his coat, and takes it off. The sun created an environment in which it was safe for the traveler to take off his coat because he no longer needed it.

If you want someone to stop being defensive, show them they don't have to be. If someone is defensive about something that happened to them in the past, let them know that you take the issue as seriously as they do, or let them know that you don't hold it against them. If someone is defensive about certain qualities of themself, show them that you are completely accepting of who they are. Remember that the way that you behave when it comes to smaller things will show someone that you are safe to trust with more serious things. It is fine if someone wants to keep parts of themself private from you, but if you validate their feelings and respect their boundaries, they might just decide that it's safe to take off their coat when you're around.

# Part 3: Advice, Pressure, and Consent

# Advice and Suggestions

We have talked a lot about the importance of listening and validating people's feelings before giving them advice. But what happens when someone *wants* advice? Imagine that a stranger came up to you on the street and said, "I'm really lost! Could you please give me some directions?" The first question you would ask is, "Where are you trying to go?" You couldn't possibly give someone directions without knowing where they want to go. Yet often, when we try to advise other people, we don't stop to ask this question. We give people directions that will take them where *we* want them to end up, or where we think they *should* end up, without regard to where the person is actually trying to go. Think about it: if you asked someone for directions to the nearest grocery store and they instead gave you directions to the nearest clothing store because they decided that your clothes were out of style and you needed a new outfit more than you needed food, that wouldn't be nice of them, and it would not have been their decision to make. When you are giving someone directions in any aspect of life, start by asking, "Where are you trying to go?"

## Word Problem

Camilla wants to paint her living room neon orange. If the surface area of the room is 800 square feet, and one can of paint covers 400 square feet, how many cans of paint does Camilla need to buy?

If your answer is that Camilla needs to buy two cans of paint, you understand how to focus on what a person is asking for help with. In this word problem, the neon orange color choice was a fixed factor, not something that was up for debate. If Camilla were to ask this question in real life, she might get a lot of responses like, "Why on earth would you choose neon orange?" even though she has already made that decision and is not requesting advice in that area.

In real life, upon hearing that your friend is painting their house, you may have helpful advice that isn't related to the measurements. Maybe you know the best store in town to buy paint. Maybe a store is having a 50% off sale on paint this weekend. This would be great information to share with your friend. But when it comes to things that a person has already decided on, like the paint color in this example, you should not try to push them to change their mind. The time to advise

113

someone on a decision that they have already made would be if you think they might be doing something dangerous without realizing it.

If someone posts a question in an online forum, you should only respond if you have an answer for the question that they are asking. Do not respond to criticize them for asking the question, and make sure you respect the fixed factors of their situation in your response. If, for example, someone wants to tell their partner about a traumatic experience they had, and they are looking for advice on how to discuss it, you should respond only if you have an answer for the question asked. If you just want to give some encouragement such as, "I hope it goes well!" that's great. But you want to avoid giving unsolicited advice such as advising the person not to share the experience at all, commenting that their partner would not want to hear about it, or criticizing the person for feeling the need to share it. The fact that they are going to tell their partner is a fixed factor of the equation, just like the orange paint in the word problem. They have already made that decision and they are looking for advice on *how* to do it. If you have that advice, or any kind words of encouragement, then you should go ahead and offer it. But if you don't have either of those, let someone else answer the question.

## Facts Are Not Problems

Sometimes it is hard to know when someone is looking for advice and when they're not. Notice the difference between these two sentences:
1. I spend a lot of time online.
2. I spend too much time online.

In the second sentence, the phrase "too much" implies that the speaker has a problem; they want to spend less time online. In this case, it would be fine to offer them tips for cutting down on their Internet time. But the first sentence does not express a problem. The person is stating that they spend a lot of time online, but they have not indicated that this is something they want to change. Often, the *way* a person says something indicates whether they are complaining about a problem or just stating a fact. If you are not sure, ask the person if something is a problem before you offer advice.

If you would respond to both of the statements above with advice on how to spend less time on the Internet, you are probably assuming that spending a lot of time online is a behavior and that a person would want to change. But think about this: If someone said to you, "I spend a lot of time jogging," or "I spend a lot of time outside in my garden," would you automatically start offering the person suggestions of how *not* to spend their time that way? What if we said things like:

"You spend a lot of time swimming? I have that problem too! I try my best not to walk by any pools or lakes, but when I find myself tempted to swim, I run to the nearest Starbucks and get a cup of coffee instead. That always calms my urge!"

"You wake up at 7:00 every morning? I used to struggle with waking up early also, but I've found that if I force myself to stay up until at least 2:00 A.M., I can usually sleep till noon. That's what you should try!"

"I notice your home is always really clean, but that's easy to fix! I just read this guide on techniques for how to avoid cleaning up when you feel the urge, and how to hold onto as many things as possible to create lots of clutter in your space. I've managed to keep my place messy ever since! Do you want to borrow the book?"

These examples may sound silly, but this is *exactly* the way we sound when we start advising people on how to fix things that they never said were problems. The only reason that advising someone on how to spend less time online doesn't sound so silly is that we apply our own biases of what people should and shouldn't do, without regard to what they *want* to do. When someone says that they normally stay up until 2:00 AM and sleep late the next morning, that does not automatically mean that they want to change their sleep schedule. When someone has a messy home with a lot of clutter, that does not automatically mean that they want to clean up or get rid of anything. When you assume these things are problems and start offering unwanted advice, you are saying, "It's not okay to be the way you are, so let me fix you."

Generally speaking, if a person *wants* to do something, they will mention it. If someone says, "I don't like onions, but I wish I could work them into my diet somehow because they're so healthy," that is a perfect opportunity to share recipes that include onions. But if someone just says, "I don't like onions," and they use a factual tone, you can reasonably assume that they do not want to eat onions. If you are uncertain about whether a person wants to change, ask the person a question such as, "Do you like your sleep schedule or do you want to be more of a morning person?" or "Do you want to organize your space, or are you comfortable the way it is?"

Exercise: List five things about yourself that you are not looking to change, but that other people often assume that you want to change without asking you:

1._____
2._____
3._____
4._____
5._____

Go over this exercise with your friends, and keep in mind that everyone you meet has qualities like these.

## Good vs. Bad Suggestions

When it comes to giving people suggestions, there are good suggestions and bad suggestions. A good suggestion is based on what someone likes or wants. A bad suggestion is based on what you think someone should do, without regard to what they like or want to do.

Good Suggestion: "You love *Harry Potter*? I bet you'll also love *The Hunger Games!*"

Bad Suggestion: "You eat a lot of peanut butter? You should switch to almond butter!"

What makes a suggestion good or bad is not about the suggestions itself; it's about *how* the suggestions are given. In the good suggestion, you are not suggesting that your friend should stop reading *Harry Potter* – you are recommending another series that your friend might like, *in addition* to *Harry Potter*. In the bad suggestion, you are telling your friend to "switch" to almond butter, which implies eating less peanut butter, or not eating peanut butter at all. Unless your friend said that they were looking for a peanut butter substitute, it is not logical to assume that someone who eats a lot of peanut butter wants to stop eating it. If you instead say, "If you love peanut butter, you might *also* enjoy almond butter," that would be okay. Good suggestions *add* to what a person likes, and are based on what you think they might enjoy. Bad suggestions *replace* what a person likes, and are based on disapproval of what they do, and what you think they should do instead. The exception is if a person tells you that they want to change their behavior, such as, "I eat way too much peanut butter – I want to cut down on it," in which case, suggesting an alternative would be good.

## Respect People's Desires

Sometimes we think that the best way to make someone feel better is to give them something positive to think about in the situation. The problem is that sometimes, when we try to be positive, we end up brushing off other people's feelings. Take this example:
Aisha: "I can't believe the bakery across the street is closing! Now I can't get my strawberry cupcakes!"
Michelle: "Maybe that's a good thing because you won't eat as many cupcakes."

The comment about eating fewer cupcakes is not a helpful statement because if Aisha *wanted* to eat fewer cupcakes, she would probably not be as upset about the bakery closing in the first place, or she might mention having mixed feelings about it. Giving this response when your friend has not mentioned anything about wanting to stop eating cupcakes is not respecting your friend's feelings and is pushing your friend to feel guilty about something that they might have felt perfectly fine about.

To further emphasize this point, imagine that Aisha said, "I can't believe the gym across the street is closing! Now I won't get to work out!" Now, would anyone say, "Maybe that's a good thing because you won't have to exercise anymore," or would everyone suggest other ways that Aisha could exercise besides going to that gym?

Aisha's reaction to the bakery closing down is *exactly the same* as her reaction to the gym closing down. If you are respectful of what matters to Aisha, your reactions to these two scenarios should be the same. If you respond differently to the gym and the bakery scenarios, you are pushing your own (or society's) opinion of what is good and bad onto your friend.

A better response to Aisha's original complaint about the bakery closing would be, "I know another bakery that makes pretty good cupcakes." This is a positive response because it is based on Aisha's actual desire. If you don't happen to know of another bakery, a good response is simply, "That's annoying" or "That sucks." Even though you cannot do anything about the bakery closing, you can still respect your friend's feelings without trying to change them.

## Happiness and Individual Needs

In order to give someone good advice, you need to listen to their problem, ask questions, and make sure that the advice you offer makes sense in their situation. When I was having a hard time in college, I got a lot of standard advice, and I tried it. I got more exercise. I walked outdoors every day. I went to meditation class. After doing those things, I felt worse. I already had almost no time to myself in college, and all those other things I did just added to my schedule of obligations. I was also living an active lifestyle already with all of the walking that I did on campus, so adding a designated time to just walk for exercise did not have much of a positive effect. I was having miserable time because there was just too much going on for me. I was much busier than I wanted to be, I was forced to interact with people almost all the time, and I had no time to just be alone and do things by myself. Strangely enough, every time I explained that this was the problem, the most common piece of advice I received was to get out more, be more social, and get more involved in different groups and events on campus. My friends, classmates, and even the school counselors advised me to make my own situation even worse. Getting out more and getting involved on campus is standard advice that people often to give to new college students. Taking this advice made me feel much worse, and getting this advice over and over again just confirmed that no one accepted what was actually wrong, which made me feel completely alone. When someone is having a problem, it is important to listen to the details of their particular situation and understand what they need, before offering advice.

It's also important to recognize that "doing well" is not going to look the same for everyone. About four years ago, I was making plans with friends or family almost every Saturday and Sunday of the year. Today, I do not make nearly as many plans with friends and family as I did back then, and I have many weekend days that I spend alone. It might look to an outsider like I was doing better when I had more social events. But the truth is, I have always loved having a lot of alone time, and I enjoy going places by myself. When I was a kid, I used to imagine how awesome it would be to be able to just hop in the car and drive to the beach by myself and not have to worry about whether anyone else wanted to come with me. Making social plans every single day of every single weekend was not normal for me. But four years ago, I had gone

118

through a breakup and felt lonely, to the point that I wanted to be with someone all the time. If I found out that my workplace was closing early on a given day, I would actually be panicking about how to fill that time, because I could not stand to be alone. If I tried to do fun things by myself, I would just end up feeling lonely, even though I used to love doing things by myself. In recent years, I've begun heal. I've regained my ability to enjoy things on my own, and as a result, I don't have as many social events on my calendar as I did right after the breakup. I'm back to the level of social activity that I desire when I'm feeling well. The fact that I was getting together with people as often as I was after the breakup was actually a sign that I was not okay. But someone who likes a lot more social time than I do might be happy having social events every day, and having fewer social plans could be a sign that they are not okay. It's important to keep mind that everyone's version of being okay is going to be a little different.

## Do You Only Tell People What They Want to Hear?

Does validating people mean that you can only tell them what they want to hear? No. Validating someone means accepting who they are and how they feel, and giving advice based on those things, not how you think they should be. For example, if you know that your friend is terrified of public speaking, and they are unknowingly planning to take a class that requires public speaking, it would be good to let your friend know. This will not be what your friend wants to hear – they might be annoyed or disappointed when they find out. But you would be doing them a favor by telling them so that they can make an informed decision about whether they still want to take the class.

When I was first out of college, I considered pursuing a career as a counselor. I discussed the possibility with my mom, and she helped me to realize that being a counselor would not be a good fit for me. We talked about how I don't really enjoy working with people, and how I absorb other people's emotions and feel drained after hearing upsetting stories. After giving it a lot of serious thought, I realized that my mom was right. I loved the *idea* of being a counselor, but it would have been a draining profession for me and it would not have left me enough energy for everything else that I want to do. This was disappointing to realize, but I was glad that my mom addressed this issue with me before I pursued a career that would not have been a good fit.

Giving someone validating advice is not the same as just telling someone what they want to hear. Validating advice means giving advice based on what you know *is* true of someone, rather than what you think *should* be true. When my mom advised me against being a counselor, she accepted who I was. If she had instead said, "Being a counselor will be good for you because working with different people all day will help you become more outgoing," that would have been invalidating advice because I had never expressed a desire to become outgoing. If my mom had disregarded the fact that being a counselor would be draining for me because she believed that a person should pour all of their energy into their career, that would have also been invalidating because she already knew that I did not want to spend my energy that way.

Validation does not mean always telling people what they want to hear. Just be sure to listen and validate someone's feelings *before* offering any advice, and make sure any advice you do offer shows that you listened, that you accept who they are and how they feel, and that you are not pushing them to be any different.

# Find an Outlet

Do you often find yourself giving advice to people who don't want it? Do you pressure people to do things that they don't want to do when you think it is best for them? Do you feel the need to fix other people's lives before you've asked them if they even have a problem or want your help? It may be that the instinct to help, advise, and take care of others is an inherent part of your personality. This can be a positive trait, but you want to make sure to use your talent where it is wanted, rather than pushing it on people who don't want it. Think about it this way: If you were a talented guitarist and lots of people loved your music, there would still be plenty of situations in which it would be inconsiderate for you to just start playing the guitar. Likewise, if your talent is advising and motivating people to change, look for an outlet where you can use this talent to help people who want your help.

If you love to motivate people, consider pursuing a career as a therapist, life coach, consultant, human resource development specialist, or anyone who gets to give advice and motivation to people who seek it. You can also pursue a career more specific to your interests: If you often find yourself pushing people to eat well and exercise, you may consider a career as a nutritionist or fitness instructor. If you find yourself telling people how to spend their money, you might enjoy being a financial advisor. If you find yourself taking over people's party plans, you could consider becoming an event planner. If a career is a long way off for you, or if you are not looking to change careers, you could consider volunteering as a tutor, coach, or mentor. Run for president of your club or captain or your team. Use your leadership skills to help people who want your help, while also respecting people who do not want you to "fix" them.

# Peer Pressure

What is your earliest memory of learning about peer pressure in school? Chances are, a teacher gave you a scenario in which a friend pressured you to do something wrong. Maybe your friend wanted you to steal candy from the drug store, try a dangerous stunt, or play a prank on an elderly neighbor. Maybe they wanted to copy off your test, or tease the new kid in school. Whenever we discussed peer pressure in elementary school, it always involved doing something that would be just as bad if you did it on your own, without being pressured. Once we got older, the peer pressure lectures became all about drugs, alcohol, and sex, but these lectures were just adults pushing us not to get involved with those things at all, rather than emphasizing our autonomy. Peer pressure was always linked to these so-called "bad" behaviors. We never learned about peer pressure on its own. We never discussed the issue of friends pressuring friends to do things that were not bad – things that might even be good – but that their friends just didn't want to do.

What determines whether pressure is positive or negative is *not* the activity that you are pressuring someone to do. It's not a matter of pressuring someone to study more vs. pressuring them to break the rules. Whether pressure is positive or negative depends on whether or not the person *wants* to do that activity. Pressuring someone to join a club that does volunteer work is not "positive pressure" just because the club itself is positive – it would only be positive pressure if the person is actually interested in joining the club, but is a little shy and wants someone to help them get involved. Likewise, pressuring someone to skip class is not "negative pressure" because you think that cutting class is bad – it is negative pressure if the other person does not want to do it. See if you can spot which of these forms of pressure are positive, and which are negative:

1.      Your friend has curly hair, and everyone agrees that she would look much more attractive if she straightened it. You've brought up the subject numerous times, and she still won't listen to you. "Come on!" you insist, "Straight hair would look so nice on you!"

2.      Your friend has been talking all summer about wanting to join the track team. When tryouts roll around, your friend says, "Maybe this was a bad idea. Everyone else is so much better than me. There's no way I'll make it!"

You tell your friend, "You've been practicing all summer and you have a great chance of making the team. If you want this, you should go for it! I know you can do it!"

3.      Your friend is very homesick at summer camp. He has secretly been using every free period to call his parents and talk to them for hours on his cell phone, even though cell phones aren't allowed. When your free period rolls around today, you tell him, "Camp is supposed to be an experience away from home, and you're not going to get that if you call your parents for every little thing! Come on, put down the phone and let's go do something fun together!"

4.      Your younger sister never cleans up her side of the bedroom that you share. Any time that you ask her to clean it, she says no. "Alright," you say, "Today we're going to tackle your side of the room. I'll help you clean up, and I'll show you how to be more organized from now on."

5.      You think your best friend would be a great addition to the school newspaper staff, but he is never interested when you bring it up. You say, "You're a great writer, you'd make a great addition to the staff, and it will look good on your resume! We'd all love it if you would join!"

6.      Your brother's friends are teasing him because he likes to knit. You say, "Your friends are being mean. If you love to knit, then you should do it!"

7.      You and your friends are walking to the ice cream shop together. By the time you arrive, one of your friends is completely out of breath. "You didn't tell me this place was so far away!" she gasps. "I didn't think it would be this much walking!"

You reply, "It was only half a mile – that shouldn't tire you out. How often do you exercise? I go for a run every morning – why don't you come with me?"

8.      Your basketball team just lost the most important game of the season, and one of your teammates is beating herself up because she missed the winning shot. She thinks the whole team must be angry with her and feels so ashamed that she wants to quit. You tell her, "Everyone makes mistakes! You are a great player and the team wouldn't be the same without you. Please don't quit. We all want you to stay!"

Answers: Scenarios 2, 6, and 8 are examples of positive pressure. The rest are examples of negative pressure. At first glance, all of these scenarios may seem like examples of positive pressure. None of them involve pushing someone to do something "bad." None of them sound like the negative peer pressure examples that we learned about in school. But if you look closely, you'll see that scenarios 2, 6, and 8 are the only situations in which the person being pressured expressed any desire to do the activity that you are pushing them to do. In the rest of the scenarios, you are pushing someone to do something that – judging by their behavior and what they have said – they do not want to do. Pushing someone to do things that they do not want to do is negative pressure.

## The Camping Trip: A Lesson in Validating People's Concerns

It was Monday morning, and Kiana and Gabby stormed into their classroom.

"Good morning girls!" said Ms. Martinez. "How was your camping trip this weekend?"

"Horrible!" Kiana exclaimed. "Absolutely horrible! Sarah ruined the trip for everyone!"

"Really? How so?" asked Ms. Martinez.

"Where do I even begin?" said Gabby, "She couldn't keep up with us on the hike – she kept complaining that her ankles hurt. So we had to stop and set up camp before we even reached the lake! When we went canoeing the next day, Sarah couldn't paddle a canoe at all so we couldn't take our usual route."

"And if that weren't bad enough," Kiana continued, "Sarah was up all night complaining about how cold and uncomfortable she was sleeping on the ground. The next morning, Sarah was crying about being homesick and my Mom took us home a day early!"

"What was she expecting?" Gabby added, "A five-star hotel? Why'd she have to come along if she was just gonna ruin it for all of us?"

"That sounds hard on all of you," said Ms. Martinez. "Where is Sarah now?"

"She's not speaking to us," said Kiana. "And frankly, I don't feel like speaking to her either after what she did!"

*　　*　　*　　*　　*

Wow. It looks like nobody had fun on this camping trip. Sarah was obviously miserable, and Kiana and Gabby feel like Sarah spoiled their good time. To top it off, this weekend has caused a fight between Sarah, Kiana, and Gabby, and everyone is upset with each other. Let's see if we can get to the root of this problem. Let's go back to last week in the school cafeteria, when Kiana was first asking Gabby and Sarah if they wanted to go camping with her family:

*　　*　　*　　*　　*

"...My mom taught me how to paddle a canoe last summer, and my brother makes the best s'mores in the world! It's gonna be such a blast!" Kiana exclaimed. "Are you coming?"

"I have to ask my parents first," replied Gabby, "But I'm definitely in!"

126

"What about you, Sarah?" asked Kiana.

Sarah fiddled with the bottle cap on her soda. "I don't know...I'm not sure about camping."

"Aw, come on!" Kiana insisted, "It'll be tons of fun!"

"I don't know..." Sarah hesitated. "I don't think I'd like sleeping outside in a tent."

"Don't be a spoilsport, Sarah. That's part of the fun!" said Gabby.

"But doesn't it get cold at night?" asked Sarah.

"Not *that* cold," said Kiana.

"Is it comfy sleeping in a tent?"

Kiana shrugged. "We do it all the time. It's never bothered us."

Sarah still looked hesitant. "How hard is the hiking part? What if I can't keep up? And don't you need strong arms to paddle a canoe?"

Gabby giggled. "Relax, Sarah! You'll be fine. Don't be such a worrywart!"

"Yeah," Kiana agreed. "We always have a great time on our camping trip. I promise you it will be fun!"

Sarah sighed. "Well, okay, if you say so."

*     *     *     *     *

Now, let's look at what happened in this conversation. Kiana and Gabby have good intentions – they think the camping trip will fun, and they don't want their friend to miss out on it. But in trying to convince Sarah to go on the camping trip when she is hesitant, they are invalidating her concerns. Sarah is trying to express issues that she may have with the trip, and Kiana and Gabby do not take her concerns seriously. They assure her that she will have a great time without listening to why she may not want to go.

Sarah goes on the camping trip and has a miserable time, and Kiana and Gabby blame her for ruining all the fun. Gabby even questions why Sarah came on the trip if she was just going to complain the whole time. But Sarah suspected all along that this camping trip was not for her, and she was invalidated when she tried to voice her concerns. Her friends convinced her that she would have a good time, regardless of any of the issues she raised. Sarah got pressured into doing something she didn't want to do, and now everyone had a miserable weekend and a huge fight. This doesn't seem like a good situation for anyone involved.

Now, let's see how this conversation *could* have gone if Kiana and Gabby had validated Sarah's feelings:

*  *  *  *  *

"…Mom taught me how to paddle a canoe last summer, and my brother makes the best s'mores in the world! It's gonna be such a blast!" Kiana exclaimed. "Are you coming?"

"I have to ask my parents first," said Gabby, "But I'm definitely in!"

"What about you, Sarah?" asked Kiana.

Sarah fiddled with the bottle cap on her soda. "I don't know…I'm not sure about camping."

"Why not?" asked Kiana.

"Well, I don't think I'd like sleeping outside in a tent," Sarah replied.

"Sleeping in a tent can be fun," said Gabby, "But it's not gonna be the same as sleeping in your bed."

"Does it get cold at night?" asked Sarah.

"Well, we dress warmly and pack lots of blankets, but it can still feel chilly," said Kiana.

"Is it comfy sleeping in a tent?"

"Well, I find it comfy enough, but Gabby is right. It's not gonna be like sleeping at home. The ground is a bit hard and we'll be sleeping really close to each other. So that's something to think about."

"Hmm," Sarah thought. "How hard is the hiking part? What if I can't keep up? And don't you need strong arms to paddle a canoe?"

"It is a bit of a hike," said Kiana. "I don't know the actual mileage, but it's about the walking distance from here to the post office. Paddling a canoe does take some practice, but we can go at a slower pace if you want to try it."

"Hmm…" Sarah thought. "I don't know."

"You don't have to come if you don't want to," said Gabby.

"Yeah," said Kiana, "I'd love for you to join us, but if you don't feel like it, that's fine too. We can always do something together another time."

"Okay. I'll think about it," Sarah decided.

*  *  *  *  *

In this scenario, Kiana and Gabby validate Sarah's concerns and let Sarah know that it's okay if she doesn't want to come. Now, let's

128

return to the Monday morning after the camping trip, and see how things are different this time around.

*    *    *    *    *

"Good morning girls!" said Ms. Martinez. "How was your camping trip this weekend?"

"It was awesome!" replied Kiana. "We went hiking and canoeing, and we stayed up late roasting marshmallows and watching the stars."

"We had a lot of fun," Gabby agreed. "I'm so glad Kiana invited me along."

"How about you Sarah?" asked Ms. Martinez. "Did you have a good weekend?"

"Yeah!" Sarah replied, "I stayed home and taught my brother how to skateboard. It was really fun!"

"Hey, maybe next weekend we can get together and do something we all like, maybe go to the park and play soccer or something," Kiana suggested.

Sarah smiled. "That sounds great!"

*    *    *    *    *

What a difference. Because Kiana and Gabby validated Sarah's feelings, Sarah was able to make the decision that was right for her, which was to skip the camping trip. As a result, everyone had a much better time, and everyone is still on good terms. It is a kind gesture to try to include people in things that you think they'll enjoy, but remember that everyone likes different things, and it is okay if something just isn't right for your friend.

An important message to take away from this story is that a lot of things are not objectively good or bad – they are good for some people and bad for others. If you went to an awesome pool party last weekend, the party might have been awesome for *you* because you love to swim and you love the friends at the party, but it may not have been awesome for someone who doesn't like to swim or doesn't get along as well with your friends. There's nothing wrong with referring to the pool party as awesome, but it's important to understand that its awesomeness is not objective, that part of what made your experience positive came from your interest in the activity.

When you present something as objectively good, it makes other people feel like they are supposed to like it, that they're just being party-

129

poopers or spoilsports if they don't. This can make it difficult for someone to say that they don't want to do something that other people expect them to enjoy, which is why Sarah had trouble saying that she didn't want to go camping. Kiana and Gabby had a hard time understanding Sarah's feelings because they treated the camping trip as objectively awesome. They didn't stop and realize that their own interest in camping was part of the reason that the trip sounded so much fun to them.

Exercise: Think of three things you absolutely love to do, things that you might automatically recommend to someone else. Then list out some of the reasons why you like these things, or why you're okay with them (ex: maybe you don't enjoy every single aspect of an activity, but the things you do love make it worth doing):

1. What you love:_____

What makes you the kind of person who would love it:

_____

2. What you love:_____

What makes you the kind of person who would love it:

_____

3. What you love:_____

What makes you the kind of person who would love it:

_____

Now practice including these reasons when you tell someone about your awesome experiences:

"Our camping trip was awesome! We did a lot of canoeing, which was great for me. I love canoeing so much that I could spend my whole day out on the lake!"

"I love my job! I have always loved cooking and the fast-paced environment gives me such a thrill!"

"My semester abroad was phenomenal! I did miss my friends, but I got to meet new people and see lots of cool sites. I've always wanted to immerse myself entirely in a new culture, so this was perfect for me!"

# Affirmative Consent

Affirmative consent means that when you ask someone if they would like to do something, they give you an affirmative "yes" answer and they sincerely want to do the activity. If you ask someone to do something twenty times, and they say no each time, but the next time you ask them, they say yes, that is not consent. That is compliance, and *compliance is not consent.* Compliance just means that the person has agreed to do something that they don't want to do because the way you're behaving towards them is worse than doing the thing they don't want to do. Imagine that a friend invites you to join a club, and you said no thanks. You friend says, "I'm going to follow you around and poke you with a stick until you agree to join my club!" They do this for a couple of hours until you finally say, "Okay, fine, I'll join your club, just stop poking me!" Would you say that you consented to joining the club?

When you keep pressuring someone to do something after they've said no, or if you try to make them feel guilty about saying no, the distress you might be causing can hurt them just as much as poking them with a stick would. If you finally get someone to agree to something after they have already said no multiple times, that is not consent. It does not mean that the person actually wanted to do the activity – it means that the pressuring, guilt-tripping, or whatever you were doing to them was worse.

Affirmative consent also means that a person needs to give a clear, "Yes, I'm definitely interested," in order for an activity to be consensual. Responses like, "Maybe," "I don't know," "I'll see," or just shrugging and not answering do not imply consent. We live in a culture where it is not always socially acceptable to just say no to things that we don't feel like doing. Think about all the times when you have said "Maybe," "I don't know," "I'll see," or just not responded. Is this how you normally answer when you are truly interested in doing something? Probably not. These are probably answers that you give in order to be polite, when you don't feel like you can just say no. (Unless you specify a reason for the "maybe," like that you need to wait until you know your schedule for the week). The same is true for other people. You should not treat a person's lack of a "no" response as a definite yes. If someone is unclear about their answer, it's perfectly fine to ask them for a definite answer, like saying, "I need to know by Friday," but the emphasis should be on needing an answer one way or another, rather than needing a "yes" answer.

Affirmative consent does not mean that everyone has to enjoy every activity, only that they freely choose to do it. If your friend agrees to pick you up from the train station at 3:00 AM, it's okay if that's not their first choice of how they'd like to spend their night – what's important is that they have decided that they are willing to help you and they do not feel pressured or forced.

## "No" Is a Complete Sentence

Here is an example of "no" used as a complete sentence:
You: "Are you coming to the talk tonight?"
Friend: "No."

For some reason, we don't always accept "no" as a complete answer to a question. We automatically expect "no" to be followed with an explanation like, "No, I'm too busy tonight." We accept "yes" as a complete sentence. If you replaced the "no" with "yes" in the above conversation, it would sound fine. You would not automatically expect someone who answers "yes" to provide an explanation of why they are attending the talk. Likewise, the answer "no" should also be accepted on its own. Unless this person explicitly promised to go the talk with you, they don't need to provide a reason or excuse for their choice. We often criticize people for making excuses, but no one would *need* an excuse if we all just accepted that "no" is a complete sentence that does not require an explanation.

## Making It Easier to Say No

Part of being consent-conscious is realizing that we live in a world where it is not always socially acceptable to say no without giving an excuse. One way to make it easier for someone to say no to something is to give them all of the information before asking for an answer. I don't like it when someone asks me if I'm free on a given day without specifying what they'd like me to do if I say yes. To make it easier for someone to say no, don't just say, "Are you free on Saturday?" Try asking a more specific question like, "Are you free to hang out together on Saturday?" or "Do you want to help me move on Saturday?" or "If I have a party this Saturday, would you be able to come?" These questions allow the person to decide whether or not they are available based on whether or not they want to do the activities that you mentioned. It is much more awkward for someone to figure out how to say no when they have already revealed that they are free on a given day.

Try to avoid conversations like this:

You: "Are you busy this weekend?"

Friend: "Nope, I'm just hanging out at home."

You: "Do you like dogs?"

Friend: "Yeah."

You: "So can you watch my dog this weekend?"

Friend: "Well...um..."

While it's perfectly fine to ask your friend for this favor, it is better to ask them for exactly what you want *first*. Your friend could be free this weekend, like dogs, and still not want to or be able to take care of your dog. But your friend might not feel comfortable just saying no without giving a reason. By asking the other questions first, you eliminate a lot of the "polite" excuses that your friend could have given, which makes it harder for them to say no. Even a simple, "Sorry, I can't this weekend," will sound strange since your friend already told you that they had no plans. Let's try again:

You: "I wanted to ask you for a favor. If you're free this weekend, would you be able to take care of my dog?"

Friend: "Sorry, I can't this weekend."

This time, the initial question was much better. It was direct and allowed your friend room to say no. Let's continue the conversation. After your friend says no, you would say:

A. "Okay, no problem."

B. "Why? What do you have going on this weekend?"

C. "That's okay. I'm sure my aunt can do it."

D. "I need to find someone and I'm not sure who else to ask."

E. "That's cool. Hey, did you see that new zombie movie?"

Choices A, C, and E are all good examples of accepting "no" as an answer. Saying, "No problem," puts your friend at ease. Changing the subject is also a good idea, as well as letting them know that you have another solution if they can't do the job.

Choice B, on the other hand can sound pushy because your friend may not have a "good reason" for saying no, and they do not need one. Choice D is not necessarily wrong – your friend may know someone else that you could ask, but it could also make your friend feel pressured into saying yes. If you do continue to discuss your dilemma with them, just be sure to make it clear that you are accepting "no" as their answer and are not hinting around for them to change their mind.

## A Positive Push Is a *Wanted* Push

There are plenty of times when you might *want* to be pushed or encouraged, even on days when you don't feel like doing anything. Maybe you have a therapist, coach, or mentor who helps to motivate you and keep you on track with your goals. This kind of encouragement is fine because it is consensual. You just want to make sure that when you push other people to do things, those people have consented to you pushing them in those ways.

Exercise: Make a list of the situations in which it is okay for someone to push you, and situations in which it is not okay for someone to push you. If you don't have any times that you want to be pushed, that is also fine.

You want to be pushed in the following ways:

_____

_____

_____

When it comes to the things you have just listed:

A. You are always open to being pushed, even if you don't specifically ask for it.

B. You will specify when you'd like to be pushed.

C. Other:_____

Who is allowed to push you?

A. Anyone.

B. Only these specific people:

_____

_____

You don't want to be pushed in the following ways:

_____

_____

_____

Ask your friends to fill out these exercises as well, so that you can share your lists with each other. Having this discussion will help to ensure that you are only pushing each other in consensual ways.

## Constructive Criticism

There are times when you need to give a person feedback on their behavior because it is hurting you or others. There are also times when it is your job to give someone feedback because you are their boss, teacher, coach, therapist, or in a position where someone has consented to getting feedback from you. But when a person's behavior is not hurting you, and when you do not have a role in their life where you need to give them feedback, any advice or criticism you give should be consensual, meaning that the other person has given you permission to give them feedback before you offer it.

Exercise: Think about areas of your life in which you would like constructive criticism and areas in which you do not want criticism. These can include things like what you eat, who you hang around with, the way you dress, what you write on your blog, how you keep your living space, how you spend your free time, the way you respond to problems in your life, the way you behave in stressful situations, or anything else that crosses your mind. First, list some areas of your life in which you are open to constructive criticism from people. (It is okay if you do not have any):

_____

_____

When it comes to the things you have just listed:
A. You are always open to constructive criticism and advice, even if you don't specifically ask for it.
B. You will specify when you'd like advice.
C. Other:_____
Who is allowed to give you constructive criticism?
A. Anyone.
B. Only these specific people:

_____

Now, list some areas of your life in which you are not open to constructive criticism:

_____

_____

_____

Go through this exercise with your friends so that you can learn about each other's boundaries regarding when it's okay to offer constructive criticism and when it's not.

If you are thinking that it is impossible to avoid being criticized altogether, that is probably true, but that does not mean that you need to contribute to the unwanted criticism in your friends' lives. If you respect your friends' boundaries when it comes to unsolicited criticism, you will help to create a culture where such boundaries are normally respected.

## Pressure and Time

A common reason people give for not being able to do things is that they do not have time or they are too busy. This reason is often criticized. My college classmates would often complain that a person couldn't possibly be too busy to do something because other people had the same amount of work and managed to make time for it. But people have different priorities. Everyone's time is their own, and if a person wants to make time for one thing but not another, that is perfectly fine.

Being too busy is not always about how much someone is doing – it can be about how much someone *wants* to be doing. People have different levels of activity that are acceptable to them, and if adding something to their schedule makes them busier than they want to be, then they are too busy to add it. Think about how you would behave at an all-you-can-eat buffet. If you just kept eating as much food as you possibly could, you would end up feeling sick. You probably feel better if you stop eating when you feel comfortably full, but not like your stomach is about to burst. Likewise, everyone has a different threshold of how much activity in their life keeps them satisfied and how much constitutes too much. If someone's free time is important to them and they would lose that free time by adding something to their schedule, they have just as much right to say that they are too busy as someone who has that time filled with an organized activity or obligation. The fact that a person *can* do more with their time does not put them under any obligation to do more.

## Pressure and Money

When it comes to activities that involve spending money, it's important to keep in mind that everyone does not have as much money as you do. If you ask someone to do something and they say, "No, that's too expensive," you should accept their answer, even if the cost is not what you would consider to be too expensive. Pressuring people further, after they have stated that they can't afford something, can make people who have less money than you feel alienated. If someone tells you that something is too expensive for them, don't cite other things they have spent their money on that you think are less important. Even if they *could* afford something (which you don't know for sure), they may be facing trade-offs that you don't have to face.

If you invite a friend to go to a restaurant and they tell you that it is too expensive for them, don't pressure them to go. If possible, you can try to find another place to go that is less expensive so that your friend can be included. If it is important to go to this particular restaurant, just accept that your friend isn't going and try to accommodate them by having the next event you plan be something less expensive. Do not say something to your friend like, "But you went to the science museum last week and that was way more expensive that this place!" Your friend might have been saving their money for a long time to go to the science museum. Your friend could have sacrificed other things because the science museum was important to them. All of the expensive things that you've seen them do could be part of a tight budget that they've planned based on their priorities, and they do not have room in their budget for this restaurant. When you don't have a lot of money, you can't afford to spend money on things that are not important to you just to go along with your friends.

When you know that some of your friends have less money than you do, try to accommodate them by planning some free or inexpensive events. It's also helpful to let everyone know the cost of an event ahead of time. Send people a link to the website of the place that you are going so that they can look at the prices and make an informed decision.

A good way to give people control over what they spend is to have everyone pay for themselves. If you go to a restaurant, everyone can pay for their own meal rather than splitting the bill evenly. If you are going to a tourist area, you can give your friends the option of packing their own lunch or buying lunch there, rather than planning to go to a sit-down restaurant. Just be sure to follow through with your original plan when it comes to spending – if you say that you're going to each pay for your own food, don't go back on that deal and decide to split the bill evenly.

# When Someone Gives You a Fake Excuse

It doesn't feel good to be lied to. It's perfectly valid to be upset when you find out that someone was dishonest about why they couldn't do something. But it's also important to keep in mind that most excuses are the products of circumstances in which it's not acceptable to be honest. When I was in college and people asked me if I would join a club or attend an event and I just said that I was not interested, they would almost always pressure me, or they would try to make me feel guilty about the fact that I was not doing it. I quickly learned that the only excuse that people deemed "acceptable" was to say that you had too much homework, so that was what I started saying. I didn't *want* to lie, but saying that I was too busy with homework was the only way that people would stop harassing me.

Even if you personally accept no for an answer, bear in mind that you may live in a culture where people don't always accept it, or where people are taught that they can't say no without making an excuse. When I was in high school, a friend invited me to a demo party. At a demo party, someone shows a bunch of products, demonstrates how they work, and at the end, you're expected to buy something. It's not what I'd call a fun party, and it was definitely not how I wanted to spend my Saturday. When I told my mom that I wasn't planning to go, she told me that I could not just tell my friend that I don't like demo parties or that I didn't feel like going – I had to make an excuse that I wasn't free that day. So that's what I did. I claimed that I had a family function that weekend. A few days later, another friend announced that she was having a just-for-fun party that I *did* want to attend on the same day as the demo party. Now, I was going to be in a huge mess because my first friend would find out that I was attending my other friend's party and that I had lied to her. Luckily for me, my second friend wanted to go to my first friend's demo party, so she ended up changing the date of her party, but I could have very easily been caught in a lie. I never wanted to lie in the first place. I only lied because I was told that I couldn't be honest about not wanting to go.

It never feels good to be lied to, but when you catch someone giving a false excuse, ask yourself, "Do I accept 'no' as a final answer? If my friend had just said that they didn't want to do this, would I have accepted it, or would I have tried to convince them to do it?" And even if you would have accepted your friend's answer in this situation, have

141

there been other times when you didn't accept their answer? Do you accept "no" as an answer in general? Do you ever complain about people not doing things that they don't want to do? (For instance, "I can't believe David didn't want to come to the beach with us! He's missing out!"). If any of these behaviors sound familiar, your friends might not feel comfortable saying no to you, which may lead them to make fake excuses. If you work on accepting "no" as people's final answer without pressuring them, people might feel safer being honest with you.

Even if you don't pressure people yourself, your friends may still feel pressured because of the culture they live in. In the case of my friend's demo party, I was not worried that this friend would pressure me, but I was told that it was not okay to just say no. When you catch someone in a lie like this, let them know that you would like them to tell the truth in the future, and assure them that you will accept their honest answer. Talk to them about why they felt the need to lie to you, and see if there is anything you can do to change that.

# My Priorities *Are* in Order, Just Not the Same Order as Yours

Validating people's feelings involves respecting their priorities when they are different from your own. It means accepting that everyone does not have the priorities that other people or society tell us to have. If someone tells you that baseball is way more important to them than school, that is perfectly fine. If someone tells you that playing computer games is more important to them than their job, that is also perfectly fine. Validation means not saying that someone needs to "get their priorities straight," because the truth is, most people *do* have their priorities in order – just not necessarily in the same order as yours.

Here are some examples of how you can respect people's priorities:

1.　　You and your friends want to take a trip on the last week of summer vacation, but one friend says they can't afford to quit their summer job a week early. You say, "That's okay. Maybe another time!" and don't push the issue.

2.　　It's your senior year of high school or college, and you are focused on applying to colleges or jobs, but your best friend isn't focused on their future at all. They are completely wrapped up in their school dance team, even though they are not planning to dance professionally. You still listen with interest when your friend talks about dance team, compliment them on their accomplishments, and cheer them on, just like you always have, without pushing them to shift their focus.

3.　　Everyone is saying that tonight is going to be the party of the year, but one of your friends wants to stay home and read a book instead. You accept their choice and don't try to convince them to go to the party.

4.　　You and your friends decide to skip play rehearsal and go to the new 3-D movie, but one friend doesn't want to miss rehearsal. You say, "Okay, have fun at rehearsal!" and don't push them to come with you.

5.　　Your friend says that they can't go to the rock concert with the rest of you because it's too expensive. You say, "Okay, no problem," and don't try to persuade them to come along, not even with a friendly-sounding comment like, "Live a little!" You also accommodate your friend by planning some free or inexpensive events in the future, so that your friend doesn't get left out.

6.　　You and your friends are having a pool party this weekend, but one friend says that they are way too busy with other obligations to go. Your other friends start badgering them about working too hard and not

143

making time for fun, but you step in and tell your friend, "That's okay, don't worry about it, maybe another time."

7. You congratulate your friend for making the honor roll. Your friend says, "Meh. My parents made me do it. I don't need school. I wish I'd spent this year at the skate park." You *don't* try to convince your friend that school is important or that they "should" be proud of their grades. Instead, you say something like, "That's annoying," or "Bummer," in response to your friend telling you that they didn't spend their year the way they would have liked to spend it.

8. Your sister doesn't want to join your family for the holidays because your mother always criticizes her about all of her life choices, and she leaves feeling bad about herself. You say, "Okay, I understand." While you would have enjoyed seeing your sister, you accept that feeling good about herself is a higher priority to her than spending the holidays with her family.

9. When talking about other people, you don't refer to things like cell phones, computer games, TV, etc., as "distractions" unless a person has specifically told you that these things are distracting them from what they would really like to be doing. Calling something a "distraction" without asking a person what they want to be focused on means that you are deciding what that person should be focused on. In reality, the thing you call "distracting" might be what the person truly cares about and wants to do, while the thing that you think they should be focused on may be distracting them from what they truly want to do.

10. You do not criticize the fact that someone is willing to sit still for hours playing video games but can't sit still to do their homework. You don't criticize anyone for being a meticulous party planner and a non-meticulous student, or for having a blog that is better written than their term paper. You accept that when people do things that they care about, they might behave differently than when they do things that they do not care about. You see these differences as reflections of the unique, dynamic people that they are.

11. Any time that you teach younger people how to make a priority list, you teach them to think about what matters to *them* and do not tell them what order to put things in. You accept that priority lists are 100% personal, so you cannot "correct" a priority list written by anyone other than yourself.

12.    When someone passes up a great opportunity that you would have taken – a job that they decided was too far away, a college scholarship in a field that they decided isn't for them, a summer internship that would have taken too much of their time – you respect their choice and do not push them to do anything differently, even if you would have taken the opportunity. (It can be frustrating to see people pass up opportunities that you would have taken, but keep in mind that if one person doesn't seize an opportunity, someone else often will. If your friend turns down a job, college acceptance, or leadership position, someone else who really wants that opportunity will probably take it. Your friend is not throwing the opportunity away – they are simply giving it to someone else who wants it or needs it more than they do).

13.    When someone tells you that a decision they are making is contingent on your behavior, you think carefully about your response and make sure that you can follow through. Imagine that you and your partner live near each other, but you both still live with your parents. You have a stable job in your hometown. Your partner has been job-hunting for a long time, but just can't find any jobs in their field within a half-hour radius of where you both live. After months of unsuccessful job-searching, your partner asks you, "If I expand my job-search range to companies that are father away, could we get an apartment together that's halfway between my job and yours?"

You want your partner to find a job, so you reply, "Sure!"

"Is that definite?" your partner asks, "Because I'm only taking a faraway job if we're moving in together. I don't want a long commute, and I'm definitely not moving farther away from you."

"Of course!" you insist. "Don't let me hold you back!"

Now, it's great that you support your partner in finding a job, but you also need to give some serious thought to the commitment you are making: Are you prepared to move in together, both financially and emotionally? Are you willing to move farther away from your family and your hometown and have a longer commute to work? These are all questions that require serious consideration. Don't just say "yes" because you think it's the right thing to do. You may really want your partner to find a job. You may think that their finding a job *should* be their top priority, even if it means a long commute or moving farther away from you. But that is not your choice to make. Your partner explicitly stated that they are only willing to consider a farther-away job if you will get an apartment together. It is essential that you give them an honest, well-thought-out answer so that they can make the choice that is right for them. Saying "yes" when you don't mean it disrespects your partner's priorities and coerces them into a situation that they do not want to be in.

Exercise: Think of a time when you did not respect someone's priorities – either by telling them what their priorities should be, or by pressuring them to make different choices. Explain what you could have done differently to respect their priorities:

_____

_____

_____

## Encouragement and Validation

Choose the answer that you would give your friend in the following scenario:

Friend: "I sort of want to try out for the play, but I'm not sure."
You'd say:

A. "Go for it! Acting is lots of fun and I'm sure you'll be great at it!"
B. "What are you unsure about?"

The more validating choice is B. Now, choice A is a good response. It's great to be supportive of your friends' interests and cheer them on. And at first glance, choice A may seem more supportive because of the optimism and encouragement. But choice A *only* shows support for your friend's potential interest in acting. Your friend mentioned that they were unsure about whether they wanted to be in the play, and choice A does not leave room for them to discuss this uncertainty. While choice A shows support, it could also brush off your friend's hesitation and make it harder for them to address their concerns. You could try mixing the responses A and B by letting your friend know that you think they'll be great at acting and have fun, while also asking them what they are unsure about.

So, you've asked your friend what they are unsure about, and they say: "Being on stage looks like fun, but I'm a little nervous about auditioning. I don't know if I'll be good enough to get a part."
You'd say:

A. "I'm sure you'll be great! If you want it, you should go for it!"
B. "You have auditions so the director can assess what role will be the best for you. They won't give you a part that you can't handle."
C. "If you audition, the worst that can happen is that you won't get in. But you're already not in the play if you don't try out, so you've got nothing to lose."
D. "I'll be in the front row on opening night, rooting for you!"

All of these answers are great choices. Since your friend has made it clear that they *do* want to be in the play even though they're scared to audition, they are most likely looking for your support and encouragement.

Now, let's change things up a bit. Imagine that when you ask your friend what they are unsure about, they say, "It's gonna be a lot of work and a huge commitment. It looks like fun, but I just don't know if I have time for it."

You'd say:
A. "Rehearsals are normally three days a week for two hours each, and more the week of the show."
B. "Why don't you talk to someone in the drama club about how many rehearsals you normally have each week?"
C. "You could always try out for a smaller part so you won't have to go to as many rehearsals."
D. "Don't worry about it! I'm doing the play and like ten other clubs!"
E. "You should go for it! You'll be great and have a lot of fun!"

In this case, A, B, and C are all good choices. Your friend needs to decide whether they have time to be in the play, so offering information is helpful, as well as offering the possible solution of a smaller part. While D and E both seem like positive, encouraging responses, they subtly pressure your friend into doing the play when your friend may not have time for it. Choice D says, "I can handle this, so you should be able to handle it too." You may enjoy being in eleven activities at the same time, but the play *alone* could be too much for someone else. The amount of time you spend rehearsing each week is objective information that your friend can use to make a decision. The fact that you are doing the play and ten other clubs is not relevant to your friend's situation, and sharing this with your friend might make them feel like the play *should* be a non-issue, when it may in fact be too stressful.

Taking people's concerns seriously creates an environment where it is acceptable for people to make different choices, while dismissing someone's concerns can create an unwelcoming environment for other people with similar issues. The standard course load for full-time students at my college was four classes per semester, but some students opted to take five classes. Whenever someone said to their friends, "I'm thinking of taking five classes next semester, but I don't know if it will be too much," everyone would immediately tell them that taking five classes was no big deal. This was an encouraging response, but it did not address anyone's concerns about five classes being too much to handle. By just assuming that their friends were fine with taking five classes, they set a standard that taking an extra class was something that everyone should be able to handle. Since I already found four classes to be too much, this standard was hurtful to me. I didn't feel comfortable sharing when I was stressed out with my schoolwork since I was "supposed" to be able to handle much more than what I was doing. One way of addressing a friend's concern would be to ask them which classes they are taking, since that could make a huge difference in their workload. You could also help your friend make a list of the pros and cons of taking the extra class. When I addressed my classmates' concerns about taking an extra class, they almost always reached the conclusion that they did want to take it, but by being open to whatever choice they made, I created an environment where they *could* have told me that five classes would be too much for them, and where other people at the table who couldn't handle five classes would not have felt like there was anything wrong with them.

When someone needs help making a decision, a good question to ask is, "What are your reasons for wanting to do this, and what are your reasons for not wanting to do this?" Most of the time, when someone thinks about this, they can figure out on their own what they want to do, and you won't need to advise them further.

# Drop the Sales Pitch

When I was apartment-hunting, I found a place that I liked. One of its major selling points was that heating was covered in the monthly rent. On my first visit to the apartment, I confirmed with the leasing agent that the heat was included, and she said "Yes" with no further explanation. Upon my second walk-through of the apartment, when I was seriously considering the place, I asked to check how high the thermostat was set, so that I could get a sense of how well insulated the apartment was. (This was during the winter). At this point, the leasing agent informed me that there was a limit on how high you could turn up your heat – the thermostat would not go above a certain low temperature. This information was not on the apartment website, and I was not informed of this on my first visit when I asked about the heat being covered. As soon as the leasing agent saw my concern, she launched into a sales pitch that the heat limit was plenty warm enough for everyone else, nobody complained about it, and she tried to redirect my attention towards other features of the apartment that I liked. The low temperature limit was a deal-breaker for me. I didn't want my attention redirected to the more positive aspects of the apartment. I didn't want to hear about how other people didn't have a problem with the heat limit. What I *did* want was to know this information upfront, on the apartment website and when I first brought up the subject, rather than to find out when I was one step away from signing the lease.

Another time, I was interviewing for a new job that I hoped would be a good fit for me. The interviewer told me right away that, even though I was applying for a job at this particular branch, I would be expected to work at another branch that was more than an hour away for part of the year. She specifically brought this to my attention because she saw my address on my resume, and she even gave me an estimate of how long my commute to the far-away branch would be in rush hour traffic. Towards the end of the interview, she informed me that my potential manager was very harsh on employees and that several people had left the job after just two weeks because of the way the manager treated them. She told me that you needed to have thick skin to work at their company, that she was used to it because her last company was even worse, and that I needed to consider whether I could handle it. She didn't ask me as an interview question whether I would be okay with this or not – she said, "You know yourself, so go home and give it some thought."

While I was disappointed to learn that the job would not work out for me, I was grateful to the interviewer for being fully honest. She was especially considerate by allowing me the time and space to think about whether I could work well in that environment, rather than asking me about it during the interview, where I would have felt compelled to give the "correct" answer and say that I would be fine. If she hadn't been upfront about these potential problems – if she had given me a sales pitch to encourage me to take the job, I would have been miserable at the company and would have quit as soon as I found another job, and it would have been much more of a hassle for everyone involved.

When a friend needs help or asks you for advice, try to think like an interviewer rather than a salesperson. While it's fine to recommend things that you think are awesome, try to avoid going into full sales-pitch mode like the leasing agent did with me. Instead of trying to pitch something to your friend and disregard their concerns, try to help your friend find what will be the best fit for them.

## Start at the Top of the Tree

An important part of being consent-conscious is leaving all options on the table and making sure that a person feels okay making any of the choices that they can make. There is a common practice of getting children to cooperate with you by offering them two choices that lead to the same result, such as, "Do you want to leave the playground now, or in ten minutes?" or "Do you want to eat your pancakes with syrup or without syrup?" By conveniently leaving out the option of skipping breakfast altogether or staying at the playground all day, the children are more likely to choose between the options you give them. I can remember times as a child when I was prepared to say no to something altogether, but went along with it simply because I was given two choices and felt compelled to pick one.

Feeling compelled to choose from the options you are given can happen at any age. One time, a new friend invited me over to play a board game. He asked me, "What do you want to do while we play? Listen to music or watch TV?" I did not want to do either of these things. I like quiet, and just playing the board game was enough stimulation for me. While my new friend did not mean to pressure me, I felt like I was supposed to pick between those two choices, so I chose listening to music, rather than saying that I preferred not to have any background noise.

Leaving out an option, acting as if a particular choice is completely off the table, is a subtle but powerful form of social pressure. Imagine that your friend is studying abroad. They were initially thrilled to leave, but now they are calling to tell you that the semester has been miserable so far. Your friend complains about various aspects of their experience, and never explicitly says, "But I definitely want to stay here." If you automatically start giving them advice on how to make the most of their experience without ever mentioning the possibility of coming home, you are subtly pressuring your friend to stay. You may not intend to do this. You may just assume that your friend wants to stay. But if you talk to your friend as if leaving is not an option, they may start to feel like it is not an option. Don't feel bad about just asking your friend, "Do you think you want to come home, or do you want to try to make it work?" You are not pushing your friend to come home, you are just leaving the option on the table.

We all have biases in terms of what we think people should do, and a common bias is that people should stick with things and not quit. While this is sometimes the best option for someone, there are also times when a person would be better off getting out of a situation that is not working for them, and they need to know that you will support them either way. If you bite into a piece of fruit and find mold growing inside, would you continue eating it in order to finish what you started? Quitting is not bad in principle, and sticking with something is not good in principle. Sometimes you need to take that first bite of the fruit before you know what's really inside.

Think of your friend's options as part of a decision tree: The most basic question of whether your friend wants to stay or leave should be at the top, and branch out into their options. Start by asking your friend:

Question 1: Do you want to stay, or do you want to go home?

A. I want to stay.

B. I'm not sure.

C. I want to go home.

If your friend answers that they want to go home, that's fine. If they are unsure, you can help them walk through their reasons for leaving and reasons for staying. If they answer that they do want to stay, go to the next most general question on the decision tree, and branch out into more options. For example, if your friend has a problem with their housing situation, Question 2 could be, "Do you want to look into a different housing option, or do you want to try to stay where you are?" If your friend wants to stay where they are, Question 3 could be about what specific issues are causing a problem with their housing. But before you reach the point of talking about these issues, be sure that your friend has established that they want to keep their housing the same. And before you even discuss housing, be sure that your friend wants to stay abroad. Starting at the top of the decision tree shows that you are open to whatever course of action is right for your friend, whereas starting too low on the decision tree automatically cuts off some of your friend's options.

Sometimes it can be hard to bring up all of the options to someone because we're worried that we will have a bad influence on them. But remember: your friend needs to do what will make *them* feel good, and the only true bad influence is influencing them in a particular direction without regard for where they want to go. If you are worried that raising the possibility of quitting might deter your friend from staying, remember that you are not pushing them in one direction or another; you are simply showing that all options are open to them.

It's great to get excited for your friends when they are looking forward to something awesome, but it never hurts to remind them that you will still support them if things don't go as planned. When everyone is expecting your friend to have a great experience, it can be difficult for them to admit that anything is wrong, and it would be helpful to let your friend know ahead of time that you won't judge them if things don't work out. If you feel like you don't want to bring up anything negative, just think of it as a backup plan. If, for instance, you tell your friend that they can stay at your place if they ever need to, it doesn't mean you *want* them to have no other place to stay – it means you are part of your friend's backup plan. Whatever your friend is doing, let them know that you'll be there for them no matter what and that you will still support them if what they are doing doesn't work out for them. You're not encouraging them to quit – you're just being part of their backup plan if they need it.

## Don't Assume Flexibility

Part of validating people is not expecting everybody to be easy-going, flexible, or to go along with things that they did not agree to do.

Exercise: Make a list of at least five things that you don't like, but that you would still be okay with: foods you wouldn't buy but would eat if someone served them to you, activities you don't like but would do if there was no better choice, things you don't like but would be willing to go along with if it was more convenient for other people:

1._____
2._____
3._____
4._____
5._____

Now make a list of at least five things you don't like that are not acceptable and non-negotiable to you: foods you would not eat even if they were the only choice on the table, activities you would not do even if the only alternative was to sit and stare at the wall, things that you would not be willing to compromise on even if it would make things easier for other people:

1._____
2._____
3._____
4._____
5._____

The purpose of this exercise is to help you understand that everyone has limits and boundaries of what they are willing and not willing to do. There is a difference between *preferring* choice A over choice B, and saying, "I am *only* okay with choice A – choice B is not an option." We all have things that fall into both categories, and it is good to understand the difference between non-negotiable things and things that are simply not your first choice, and to not assume that everyone will go along with everything. This is a great exercise to share with your friends, so that you can learn about each other's limits.

Imagine that you promised to hang out with a friend on Saturday, but later, a bunch of your other friends invite you to a party on the same day. You may think the solution is to invite the first friend to the party with your other friends, and then you haven't broken your promise to hang out with them. This definitely *could* be a great solution, *if* your friend wants to go to the party, but you should not automatically expect your friend to do something that was not part of the plan. You can definitely ask your friend if they'd be interested in the party, but the way you ask should make it clear that it's perfectly okay if they don't want to go:

Instead of: "My friends are having a party this Saturday, but I asked and they said you could come."

Try: "Would you be interested in going to my friends' party together this Saturday? If not, that's totally fine and we can stick with our original plan."

Your friend might be psyched about going to a party together, but they also might have only been interested in spending time with you alone. If you *only* give your friend the option of going to the party with you when they don't want to go, you are breaking your promise to hang out with them, the same as if you had gone to the party without inviting them.

There are times, of course, when plans have to change. Maybe there is a thunderstorm the day that you planned to go to the beach. When this happens, make sure that everyone knows the new plan ahead of time so that they can make an informed decision about whether they still want to go. Be aware that everyone who agreed to go to the beach will not necessarily be interested in doing something else, and that is okay. If the plans need to change when people are already at the event – for instance, if it starts raining when you get to the beach or if you arrive at your destination and find that it's closed – try to make sure your new plan accommodates everyone's needs. If you were planning to do something free or inexpensive, don't decide to do something that costs a lot more. If you were planning to do something relaxing, don't pick a new activity that is physically strenuous. If anyone has dietary restrictions, mobility limitations, sensory issues, or other things that were accommodated in your original plan, be sure that the new plan also accommodates everyone. Above all, make sure to *ask* everyone individually if the new plan works for them.

Be cautious about changing plans when someone does not have the option to leave. If your friend is staying with you and your family on a weekend trip far from home and they do not have their own car, they do not have the option of changing their mind and going home if you decide to do something radically different from what you had told them you'd be doing on the trip. Anytime someone is not able to walk out of the situation, it is important to communicate clearly with them about what the trip will be like before it happens, and stick to that plan as best you can. Even if you and your friends are just on a daytrip, but you are hours from home and came in the same car, be sensitive to the fact they don't have an easy option to leave.

Finally, if someone is counting on you for something important, always ask and do not assume that they will be okay with something different than what you agreed to. If you promised your friend that you would get an apartment with them, but some of your other friends have a townhouse and say that the two of you can move in, *ask* your friend if they are interested in the offer, and make it clear that it's okay if they are not. Your friend might be excited to live in the townhouse, but they also might *only* want you as their roommate. Keep in mind that your friend might have made decisions based on your promise to live with them. If your friend only wants one roommate or only has specific people they are willing to live with, they may have turned down other housing offers that would have worked for them because they already made a promise to live with you. They might have accepted a job offer only under the assumption that they could get an apartment with you in a particular location. You can present the offer of living in the townhouse with other people, but let your friend know that you will keep your promise to live with them no matter what they decide, and that it's perfectly okay if they are only interested in your original plan.

# Be a Validating Host

When you say that an event is open to everyone, you are making a commitment that everyone is welcome at the event, including people of different skill levels, knowledge levels, and levels of commitment and involvement. While you can't control individual people's behaviors towards each other, you need to really consider – and discuss with your event cohosts – what "open to everyone" means in terms of how you will treat people.

"Open to everyone" means open to people of varying skill levels. One year at my college, the astronomy club had a stargazing event, and they said that everyone was welcome. When my friend attended this event and did not know how to use a telescope, a member of the astronomy club made fun of her and said, "You're like a five-year-old!" While it's not nice to insult someone in any case, it is a betrayal of trust label an event "open to everyone" and then treat someone this way. Most people would assume that "everyone" includes people who have never used telescopes.

If you are holding a discussion which "everyone" is welcome to attend, "everyone" should include people who do not know the latest news, trends, or issues regarding the topic, and who do not know insider jargon. If you are hosting a discussion that is open to everyone, you should be prepared to answer questions and explain concepts in detail to people who have no prior knowledge, without putting anyone down for what they do not already know.

Additionally, being welcoming to non-regulars means accepting that everyone who attends your event is not necessarily looking to become more involved beyond that event. While it's fine to invite people to join your organization, an event that welcomes everyone should not involve pressuring people to join, spending a lot of time complaining about not enough people being involved, or making people feel guilty if they don't want to get involved beyond this one event. While it can be tempting to try to push people to join a group that you are passionate about, keep in mind that you probably want members who interested enough to join without being pressured. It's better to have a smaller group of people who are committed than a larger group of people who don't really want to be there.

Keep in mind that every event does not have to be for everyone. There is nothing wrong with having an event that is just for people who know how to use telescopes, people who are knowledgeable about an issue, or people who are passionate about a cause. Sometimes you need to be with other people who you don't have to explain things to, people who already get it. It's just important that you clarify that in advance, by stating that some level of experience or knowledge is expected, or labeling your gathering as a recruiting event. You don't want to label an event as "open to everyone" when it is not.

Another time that you have more power than another person, or more of a say in what happens, is when the other person is a guest in your home. When another person is out of their comfort zone while you are in yours, they may feel obligated to go along with what you want to do. If a far-away friend or family member is staying with you, it's a little bit harder to simply ask them, "What do you want to do?" since they are probably not familiar with the area and their options. A good way around this issue to give your guest choices. Offer a number of different options for what to do, and let them choose. Remember that if you ask, "Do you want to go the concert tonight, or would you rather hang out at home?" it's easier for your guest to choose staying home than if you just asked, "Do you want to go to the concert tonight?"

Even if someone is not a guest staying in your home, there are other situations where you have more power than someone else because you are more closely connected to a group, such as if you invite a friend or partner to your family event, or if you invite a friend to do something with a group of friends who already know each other. When you invite someone to do something with people they don't know, try to make them feel welcome, like you would if they were a guest in your home. If all your friends from computer club want to talk about coding and you can see that your non-computer-club friend whom you invited along is bored and left out, you should try to steer the conversation in a different direction. Your friend may not feel comfortable speaking up when they are outnumbered by people who want to talk about coding. If your partner comes to your friend's birthday party with you and has any kind of a problem, such as feeling sick, make sure to help them. Your partner may not know anyone else at the party well enough to ask for help.

When you are in a position of power because you are closer to the group than your guest is, you may need to take extra steps in order to be consent-conscious with your guest. To understand how these power dynamics work:

159

Imagine that you and your partner are going to a family barbeque with your partner's extended family. The two of you have already decided that you will stay at the cookout for the afternoon, and then you will spend the evening together just the two of you. You are looking forward to spending the evening alone with your partner. When it gets to be about the time that you had planned on leaving, your partner's grandmother says, "Why don't you two stay for dinner?" The rest of the family agrees that they'd like you to stay. Your partner says, "That's fine with me," then turns to you and says, "Are you okay staying?" Technically speaking, they did *ask* you if you wanted to stay rather than telling you, but would you honestly feel okay saying no to their grandmother when their whole family wants you to stay? Probably not. Probably, you would feel obligated to stay even if you didn't want to. This is important to keep in mind when it's *your* family event. If a member of your family asks if the two of you want to do something that you hadn't planned on, and you don't think your partner would feel safe being honest in front of everyone, it's better not to reveal how you feel until you've discussed it with your partner. You could say something like, "Maybe," or "We'll see," and then find a private moment with your partner to ask them what they want to do. (If this issue comes up a lot, you could have a plan in mind, like that you'll ask them to grab something from the car in order to get a moment alone). If your partner's answer is no, tell your family that you two have decided *together* that you'd prefer to do something else, as in, "I think we're going to head home," rather than, "Johanna wants to head home," which would put Johanna on the spot and might lead to your family pressuring her to stay. (If this kind of issue comes up a lot, it may be helpful to have separate rides home). When you are the person with the greater connection to the group, it is easier for you to say no than it is for the person who is less connected.

Even when you don't have a stronger connection to a group than your friend does, keep in mind that asking someone a question in front of other people can lead to social pressure. If your friend is having a party and you want to ask if you can bring along another friend, it would be better to ask your friend privately than to write a public message on the Facebook event page, where all of the other guests can see your question. Even if you don't mean to pressure your friend, your friend might feel pressured to say yes because other people are watching. Your friend might know that other friends will judge them if they say no. Posting the question publically also allows everyone else to get involved in the conversation. Other people could comment that they can't wait to see the person you'd be bringing along before your friend has a chance to respond, which adds to the pressure for your friend to say yes. If your friend says no, other guest could leave comments such as, "What's the big deal?" or "Don't be such a drag!" and leave the host feeling outnumbered. Keeping the conversation private reduces the social pressure, and makes it easier for your friend to answer honestly.

Keep in mind that it is okay to not invite everyone to every event. While it is not nice to purposely exclude someone to make them feel left out, it's perfectly fine to just invite your computer club friends over so that you can talk about coding all you want. It's good to spend time separately with different people so that you can enjoy talking about the interests you have in common. It's fine to not invite someone to a family event because you want to spend quality time with your family and don't want to have to host someone and worry about their needs. Before you invite someone to an event where they won't know the other people, think about how you were planning to behave at the event, and ask yourself how that will be different if you invite another person along. Is the friend you're thinking of inviting normally comfortable mixing in and meeting new people, or will they want to stick by your side all day? Are they normally comfortable speaking their mind with new people, or will you need to check with in them? Will you enjoy spending the time with this friend, or will you feel like they are interfering with you spending time with other people at the event? Discuss potential issues with your friends ahead of time, and know that it is okay if you can't invite everyone to everything.

## Consent-Conscious Touching

When I was a kid, my friend almost drowned at a pool party. We were all fooling around, when someone pushed my friend into the deep end of the pool, not realizing that she couldn't swim. She was okay, but very shaken. Our parents referred to this incident as an "accident." While it was certainly an accident in the sense that we didn't mean to put our friend in danger, it was not an accident that we all thought it was okay to push someone into the pool without their consent. It was not an accident that we all grew up in a culture where everyone considers certain non-consensual activities to be perfectly acceptable. It was not an accident that even after this incident, not one adult told us that we should ask a person's permission before pushing them into the pool.

This doesn't mean that you can't fool around and have fun with your friends. It's just good to ask ahead of time if everyone wants to play that way. All you have to do is ask, "Do you want to wrestle?" "Do you want to have a tickle fight?" "Do you want to push each other into the pool?" and see if the other person says yes. That's all it takes. Then you can have fun together. Some people will act like it's an annoyance to have to ask first, but really, it's just treating touching the same way we treat everything else. If you want to go for a walk with someone, you don't normally just grab their hand and drag them outside – you ask them if they'd like to go for a walk with you.

It's common to call someone a "bad sport" if they don't like it when you drag them into something like tickling or pushing them into the pool. But a person can't be a bad sport if they never agreed to play.

In the case of the pool, it's good to always ask someone if they want to play that way so that you don't catch them off-guard. Even a strong swimmer can get hurt if they are not prepared. In the case of things like wrestling or tickling, your friends might tell you that they like being tickled or that it's okay for you to hug them or touch them in certain ways without asking first. That's totally fine, but until you have talked about it, you should ask.

Remember when we said that affirmative consent means that you need to have a definite "yes" answer, and that not getting a clear response means no? The same is true when you start touching someone without asking. Just because a person does not give you a clear, affirmative "no," does not mean that they want you to keep touching them. It's the same way that when someone says, "I don't know," or just shrugs and says nothing when you ask them if they want to do something, it usually means they are not interested. The difference is that you have a lot more power over someone when you are physically with them. If you pressure a friend into going someplace with you next weekend, they can still back out of it by making up a reason why they can't go, or by just not showing up. But when you are physically together and you just start touching someone, it is not always easy for the other person to say no or to get up and walk away. It is especially important that you ask and discuss the kinds of touching that you and the other person are okay with. Even after someone has told you that it's okay to touch them in certain ways without asking first, always stop if they tell you to stop, or stop to check in if they seem hesitant or uncomfortable.

## Sex and Affirmative Consent

[Content: sexual assault]

If you are involved in a sexual relationship with anyone, affirmative consent means:

1.      *Asking* people whether they would like to do sexual things with you, and accepting their answer.

2.      Not doing sexual things to people unless they have explicitly said that they would like to do those things with you. This includes any kind of sexual touching, making sexual comments, and sending sexual emails or texts.

3.      Accepting that people can dress however they want, be friendly, flirt with you, or dance with you, and that does not mean they owe it to you to have sex.

4.      Not doing anything sexual to someone who is drunk, asleep, or otherwise unable to give consent.

5.      Not tricking people into doing sexual things with you, such as sending you pictures or videos, when those people don't understand that you are looking at them in a sexual way.

6.      Not pressuring people to do sexual things with you, even in a seemingly friendly way, like, "Come on, you got me turned on!" The fact that you have started doing sexual things with someone does not obligate them to do things that they do not want to do.

7.      Understanding that some people may feel pressured to give you what you want, even if you aren't trying to pressure them, and being sure that everyone honestly wants to do what you're doing. (This is especially important to pay attention to if the other person is less assertive than you).

8.      Respecting everyone's right to change their mind after they've agreed to something, or to opt out of sexual activities once you've already started, no matter what point you're at.

9.      Not doing sexual activities with people whom you have power over, such as an employee, even if the other person initiated.

Yes means yes. Not fighting back or resisting does not mean yes. You only have the right to do sexual things to someone if that person has explicitly given you permission. If someone wants to have sex with you, they should be *actively engaged*, not just going along with what you want them to do.

The most important rule is to ask first. Imagine that your friend calls and asks if you want to eat at a restaurant that you hate. On the phone, you could probably tell your friend that you don't want to eat there. Now, imagine that you're already in the car with your friend, and without asking you, your friend pulls into the restaurant parking lot, gets out, and just expects you to follow them inside. How would you react in this case? Would you feel just as comfortable saying, "No, I don't want to eat here," as you would have on the phone? Or would you feel like you had to go along with what your friend wanted? This is what it's like when you just start touching someone without asking. You put them in the position of feeling pressured to go along with something because it has already started, rather than giving them an easier option of saying no. If when you ask, the other person seems uncertain of their answer, just say, "That's okay," and ask if they'd like to do something else instead.

A person must be mentally aware in order to actively agree to something. If you broke into someone's home and robbed them while they were asleep, you would never get away with saying that it was okay to steal because the sleeping person didn't do anything to stop you. The same would be true if you stole someone's wallet out of their pocket while they were drunk, sick, or passed out. You would never think that it was "okay" to take their wallet without asking just because they were too drunk to stop you. Likewise, you can't have sex with someone who is drunk, asleep, passed out, or for any reason unable to give consent. The person must *actively* want to have sex with you.

Secondly, *you* need to be mentally aware in order to know whether someone else wants to have sex with you. It would be wrong to drink before you drive, operate heavy machinery, perform surgery, or anything else that might lead to someone getting hurt. If you are so drunk that you are unable to understand whether someone else wants to have sex with you or not,
or that you don't have enough self-control to stop doing something when someone tells you stop, then you are not aware enough to be doing sexual things at all.

The only thing that matters is whether or not a person actually says that they want to have sex; anything else that you perceive as asking for sex – clothing, dancing, flirting - has nothing to do with actual consent. If you guess that someone wants to have sex and you are wrong, that is not the other person's problem. You would not go up to someone in a football uniform and start tackling them, or someone in a wrestling uniform and start wrestling with them because they "looked" like they wanted you to do those things to them. A person is only consenting if they actually say that they want to have sex with you. A person's clothes, dancing, or flirtatiousness do not mean that they want to have sex with you. There is no room for confusion because if you don't know what someone wants, you ask them.

Treat sexual activities like any other activities in terms of not assuming what people want. Imagine that a friend invited you to hang out, but when you got to their house, they said, "Ready to go skydiving?" You had no idea that they expected you to go skydiving. You're terrified at the thought of it, but your friend is acting as if you already committed to doing it, as if "hang out" was code for "go skydiving," and you should have known what they meant. This often happens with sexual activities – one person was supposed to understand that the other person invited them over to have sex, when the other person never said so. Of course, you still have the right to say no, but it's easy to pressure another person into having sex by implying that they already promised they would. Don't assume that because someone says yes they'll hang out with you or go on a date with you, it means that they will want to have sex with you. Ask for what you want instead of talking in code.

Even if someone did say they would have sex with you, a person can change their mind at any time, no matter what. If your friend promised to go to a movie with you, but then decided that they didn't want to, you might feel disappointed. But would you ever think that you had the right to drive to their house and physically force them into your car, or threaten to hurt them if they didn't come to the movie with you? Probably not. Probably if you did either of these things, everyone would recognize that what you did was wrong, even if the other person had originally said they would go. This is not an excuse when it comes to sexual assault – it doesn't matter what someone said earlier if they are saying no right now.

# Yes Means Yes

Imagine that you're having a party tomorrow. You created the Facebook event two weeks ago and invited 50 people. You go online to see how many people responded, and the guest list today reads as follows:

10 Attending

5 Maybe Attending

5 Not Attending

30 (No Response)

Based on this information, how much food are you planning to buy for this party? How many people do you expect will come? Take a moment to think about it.

You probably estimated somewhere between ten and fifteen guests. But the question is: Why aren't you preparing for forty-five guests? Only five people out of fifty actually *said* that they weren't coming, so doesn't that mean that you should be prepared for forty-five people to show up?

You probably won't prepare for forty-five guests because you know that you're not going to have forty-five guests. Regardless of how many people responded "no" on Facebook, you *know* that the majority of people who did not specifically say that they were attending are probably not going to attend. If you understand this concept, if you know enough not to waste your money buying food for those thirty people who didn't respond, then you understand that not responding "yes" means no. You understand affirmative consent.

Affirmative consent is not a radical concept. It's not an extra-special, above-and-beyond way to treat someone. This is how we communicate *all the time*. In most of our interactions, an enthusiastic yes means yes. "Maybe," "I'll see," or no response all mean no. "Yes means yes," is not just an idealistic standard – it is the way things actually work. Just look at your interactions with people and you'll see it.

You have more power over someone when they are physically with you than when they have the option of staying home. You have more power when the activity itself is something that is easy to force on someone – it would be hard to physically force someone to go jogging with you if they don't want to, but it's easy to start sexually touching someone without their consent. And most importantly, sexual touching

167

is intimate and involves a lot of very strong feelings, and pushing someone to do that when they don't want to is a huge violation of boundaries and will hurt the person much more deeply than if you pressured them to do anything else that they didn't want to do. For that reason, you need to always make sure that a person wants to do sexual things with you before you start doing them. Ask people what they want, *let them know* if you are getting "mixed signals" and are unsure what they want, and accept that if someone doesn't seem interested, then the answer is no.

# Power Dynamics

[Content: examples of abuse of power]

Even if you have no intention of pressuring someone into doing things that they don't want to do, you can still inadvertently pressure them based on the power dynamics that you have. When you have some kind of social power over someone, such as being their parent, teacher, boss, or even just being older, more experienced, or more confident than them, the other person can easily feel like they have to do whatever you request or suggest.

My mom used to be the CFO of a company. When she and her department wanted to go out to lunch together, they would all suggest different restaurants. My mom found that whenever she made a suggestion, everyone automatically went along with the restaurant of her choice. Even though my mom had no intention of making this decision for the group, her employees felt like they had to agree to whatever she suggested. After this happened a few times, my mom stopped suggesting a restaurant and said that wherever other people wanted to go was fine. My mom knew that, while she was in charge of what went on at her office, she should not decide for the group where to eat lunch, and she did not want to use her power that way. Even when you have no intention of pressuring others, sometimes your power dynamics cannot be undone.

If you have a position of power over someone, such as being their teacher or supervisor, it is important to remember that they may feel required to do things that you ask outside of work or school because of this relationship. If you need a personal favor – for instance, you need help moving into a new home – you should only ask people who would feel comfortable saying no. If you invite your employees or your students to help you move – even if you truly consider it optional and are not planning to treat anyone differently as a result – these people might feel obligated to help you because you control their paychecks or their grades.

In one of my college classes, our professor wanted the class to be filmed for a TV segment, but we all needed to consent to the filming. Our professor gave us the email address of a different person in the department and told us to email that person if we did not want the class to be filmed. The second person would only inform our professor of whether or not everyone consented to the filming, but would not

169

mention any names. This is a good example of how to handle consent when there is an imbalance of power. Our professor understood that we might worry that she would hold it against us if we said no to the filming, so she figured out a way for us to be anonymous. The only improvement I would add is that it would have been better if we all needed to tell that second person that we *did* consent to the filming, rather than only emailing her if we had a problem.

Pursuing an intimate relationship with someone whom you have power over is not a good idea – the person may feel pressured to do what you want them to do because of your position of power, even if you have no intention of pressuring them. If you want to pursue an intimate relationship with someone that you have *questionable* power dynamics with – for instance, someone who used to work for you but no longer does, or a peer that you tutored or mentored in the past – you need to be sure that the other person feels on equal ground with you. Begin your relationship with lower-stakes activities. High-stakes activities would include doing romantic or sexual activities – activities where someone could be hurt and violated if they get pressuring into doing things that they don't want to do. Before doing high-stakes activities, try going to a movie or meeting for lunch, and see how the other person reacts. Do they treat you like an equal in terms of deciding what movie to see or where to eat, or do they automatically go along with what you want? If you know them well enough, you can test this by suggesting something that you know they won't like, and seeing if they are honest about it. Before doing anything intimate with the person, do lots of less intimate activities to establish that the person is treating you like an equal and will feel perfectly comfortable saying no to things that they don't want to do.

Some power dynamics, like being someone's boss, are clear-cut and easy to recognize. Other times, you have to look more closely to realize the power that you have over someone else. Imagine that you have a lot of friends. You are popular among your peers, and you feel confident in yourself. You rarely have a problem expressing your opinion, even if it goes against the group. You often fall into a leadership role with your friends and are usually the one to suggest plans and organize fun events. Then, you meet Melanie, who is shy and doesn't have many friends. You and Melanie get to know each other and hit it off right away. You introduce Melanie to all of your friends, and she seems eager for them to like her. You tell Melanie that you're in the chorus and the robotics club, and she joins both activities along with you. Melanie goes along with whatever you and your friends want to do and never says anything that goes against the group. You've really taken Melanie under your wing and helped her to fit in and find friends, and she appreciates it.

Now, you may feel as if you and Melanie are on equal ground. You're the same age, and you don't have a position of authority over Melanie. Yet, you have more social power than Melanie does. You're more popular. The fact that Melanie met all of her friends through you could create an unequal power dynamic where if the two of you have an argument, your friends might automatically take your side since they knew you first. If this is the case, Melanie might be aware of this and be afraid to stand up to you, knowing that she would have no support if you got mad at her. You're also more confident and have more ability to make your own choices. You joined activities that truly interested you, while Melanie followed your lead. This could mean that Melanie will automatically follow your lead and would feel uncomfortable saying that she doesn't want to do what you suggest. You may be peers, but this power dynamic could be as unbalanced as if you were Melanie's parent.

The most important thing in a case like this is to understand what's going on. Does Melanie have any friends who would support her if she got into a fight with you? Does Melanie freely give her own input, disagree with you, and say no to things that you suggest? Since Melanie is less confident than you, you can make an extra effort to ask for her ideas, suggestions, and opinions, and try to make sure that you do what Melanie wants to do some of the time. If Melanie defers to you on everything, you could say something like, "I picked last time, so you can pick this time." Or ask a question like, "What do you think of our new principal?" and let Melanie answer before offering your opinion. Show Melanie that you've listened and respect her opinion, even if you disagree. You could say something like, "Well, I don't like her as much as our old principal, but you make a good point – her new tutoring program has helped a lot of students!"

Be sure to establish an equal power dynamic with Melanie on smaller things before you move into higher-stakes activities. Does Melanie feel free to disagree with you? Has she ever said, "No thanks,

I'm not into that?" Make sure she can freely disagree with you on lower-stakes activities before you do anything more intimate with her. One green flag to look for is to see if when Melanie agrees with you, she adds any opinions of her own to the conversation. For instance, if you ask Melanie if she wants to get Chinese food from your favorite restaurant, does Melanie just say, "Yeah, that sounds good," or does she add anything like, "That sounds great – they make the best eggrolls!" Adding her own opinion to the mix is a good sign that Melanie is truly interested, rather than just going along with what you asked.

If you want to check how comfortable Melanie feels saying no, ask her about something that you know she doesn't want to do. If you know that Melanie hates ice skating, ask her if she's interested in ice skating with you and see what she says. Melanie should be perfectly comfortable saying no to ice skating *before* you try activities like truth or dare, anything intimate or sexual, or anything that could put Melanie way out of her comfort zone (such as going away with your family for a whole weekend). Do not move into higher-stakes activities if there is any uncertainty about Melanie's ability to say no to you.

An important question to ask yourself in all of your relationships is: Do I have more ability to hurt this person than they have to hurt me? If you hit a child, you can obviously hurt them much more than they would hurt you if they hit you. If you call a child stupid, that will emotionally hurt them much more than if a child called you stupid. While the child would probably be punished more harshly for doing these things to an adult, the real consequences are much more severe if an adult does these things to a child. To be consent-conscious, you should always step back and ask yourself, "Is this a fair fight? Can the other person do the same damage to me that I could do to them?" If the answer is no, whether because you're older than them, because you have actual authority or control over their life, because the other person is desperately seeking your approval more than you're seeking theirs, because the person cares more about having relationship with you than you care about having one with them, because you're more confident, because the other person just has a hard time standing up for themself, or because the other person is just hurt more easily than you, you do not have equal power dynamics, and you need to take extra care to ensure that you have a consent-conscious relationship.

These are some of the types of power that you can have over someone:

Physical Power – When doing physical activities such as wrestling, playing rough, or any sexual activities, you may have a physical advantage over someone else if you're stronger than they are. When doing physical activities with someone who is much smaller or less strong than you, it is extra important to be consent-conscious and to realize that the person may not be able to physically get away from you when they want to. Keep checking in to see if the other person is doing okay, and as always, be sure to stop when the other person asks you to stop.

Mental Power – Sometimes you have more mental ability than another person. This is especially true between adults and children. You may have more knowledge and understanding of how things work than the other person does, making it easier for you to take advantage of them. You may have an easier time lying to someone and getting them to believe you. When you have more mental power than someone else, take extra care to make sure that you are not taking advantage of the other person, and share your knowledge with them.

Emotional Power – Sometimes you are able to hurt another person emotionally more than they could hurt you. Again, this is especially true with adults and children – parents can hurt their children's feelings much more easily than most children can hurt their parents' feelings. If a child gets upset and tells their parents, "I hate you and I never want to see you again!" that might hurt their parents, but not as much as if the parents said the same thing to their child.

Other times, you can have emotional power over a peer whose feelings happen to get hurt more easily than yours do, or a friend who has more of a stake in your relationship than you do. For instance, your friend could care so much about your friendship that they would stay with you if you started treating them horribly, whereas you would be able to walk away from the friendship if they started treating you horribly. Be sure to fight fair, don't purposely attack someone over something that they are sensitive about, and be extra sensitive of the other person's feelings when you are not on equal ground.

Economic Power – You have more power economically when you have some control over the other person's financial situation. This is true for parents and children, employers and employees, and in relationships where you and your partner combine your income and expenses. You have a lot of power over someone when they can't get out of a relationship with you because they can't afford to live on their own. This is something to be aware of in your relationships, especially if you make more money than your partner: Is your partner worried that you might kick them out of your home? Do they feel unsafe bringing up issues that might upset you because of this fear? While you may not be able to change your partner's financial situation, make sure that you do not take advantage of it.

Social Power – You have social power when you are more popular than another person – when you both know that if the two of you had a fight or stopped being friends, everyone would take your side because you have more social capital, even in a case where you did something wrong. When this happens, try to keep your issues with the person as private as possible. It's okay to talk to someone else if you need support, but, unless the person has done something really horrible to you, try your best not to turn everyone against them when you know that you have more social power than they do. If other people say bad things about people who have less social power than you, you can use your social power to stand up for them.

# Part 4: Self-Understanding

We've talked a lot about how to validate other people's feelings. In this section, we will discuss how to apply the same principles to your own life, to help you do what is right for you in spite of social pressures.

# Goal-Setting

Setting and achieving goals requires a lot of validating yourself: saying, "This is me, this is what I want, this is how I work best, and that's okay!" A lot of the ways that we are taught to achieve goals do not take people's individual needs into account. For instance, if you spend all of your time with a structured routine, you may not have the chance to discover that you're much happier with lots of free, unstructured time. If you go searching for advice on how to achieve a specific goal, you will often get standard advice that does not necessarily work for everyone.

One common piece of advice is that if you want to exercise more, you should get a workout buddy. This advice assumes that everyone enjoys being social, and that having another person to exercise with will make you enjoy the workout more. But just as some people aren't always in the mood to exercise, some people aren't always in the mood to socialize. Some people would much prefer to exercise alone, and adding a buddy to the mix could make them less interested in working out. The workout-buddy advice also assumes that everyone is okay with having a friend motivate them to exercise on days when they don't want to, when this could put a strain on the friendship. I personally would not stay friends with someone who pushed me to exercise when I didn't feel like it, no matter what my goals were. Like most advice, a workout buddy is a great idea for *some* people, but not all people.

So, what are some good goal-setting tips that work for everyone? The best way to achieve your goals is to figure out what works best for you personally, even if that is different from what you have been taught to do.

Here are some tips to help you get started:

1.	When you choose a goal, make sure it is something that you personally want to achieve, not just something that you've been told to do or something that you feel like you are "supposed" to do.

That said, if your parents say you can't stay on the wrestling team unless you improve your grades, even though you don't care about your grades, it may be worth working to improve them. Just keep in mind what you're doing it for. Remember also that your reasons are your own – no one else can tell you what is a good reason or bad reason for accomplishing a goal.

2.        Think about the reason you want to accomplish your goal. If, for instance, your goal is to wake up earlier, what is the reason behind it? Do you want to make sure you get to work or class on time? Do you have specific activities that you are trying to squeeze into your morning before you leave? Or do you just want more time to relax in the morning so that you don't feel rushed out the door? Knowing what you really want will help you figure out the best approach. Stay open to different ways of achieving the same result. If you find that waking up earlier just isn't working for you, you could try doing more preparation the night before, which would give you more time in the morning without having to change what time you wake up.

3.        Decide how important your goal is to you and where it falls with the other things that matter to you. You can think about concrete activities, such as knowing that you're more committed to anime club than to soccer, but you should also consider more general things, such as spending time with friends and family, maintaining your physical, mental, and emotional well-being, and just being happy and feeling good about yourself. You may not think of these things as goals, but they can be just as important to you, if not more important, than your other goals. What will you do if a friend invites you to do something fun together when you had planned to work on your goal? What if your new music teacher is really hard on you and makes you feel bad, but you know you'll learn a lot from them? What if you believe in your volunteer club's mission, but you just don't get along with the other members? What if it's important to you to share personal things on social media, but this will make your acquaintances less likely to recommend you for jobs? Different people will give you different advice on these dilemmas, but deciding ahead of time where your goal fits in with other things that matter to you will make you feel better about your choices. Also, establishing what matters most to you will help you to determine which strategies work best for you. For instance, if your emotional well-being is at the top of your list, then a goal-keeping strategy that leaves you feeling bad is not something that "works" for you, regardless of how much work you accomplish on your goal. Remember that it's okay to

set goals that are not at the top of your list. Every single thing can't be your top priority at the same time.

4.      In order to reach a goal, it's good to experiment with different methods to learn how you work best. (You will find more details on that in the next section). As you experiment, pay attention not only to how much progress you make on your goal, but also on how you feel as you are doing it. For instance, if your goal is something that you are passionate about, you should continuously check in not only on your progress, but also on whether you are maintaining the passion that you started with. In the long-term, maintaining your interest in something is just as important as making progress. If you are getting a lot done, but you are using a method that makes you resent something you used to love, you may eventually lose interest in the goal altogether. Even if your goal is something that you are not passionate about, you are more likely to continue with it if you use a method that makes you feel better about it, rather than worse.

5.      Remember that success can mean anything you want it to mean. Success does not have to be related to an organized activity, your education, or your career in order for it to "count." If you want to be a good parent, sibling, friend, or romantic partner and you continuously work on those relationships, that is a kind of success. If you want to feel more comfortable doing something that used to scare you and you do it, that is a kind of success. If you just want to have a super fun summer and you do it, that is a kind of success as well. Success can be absolutely anything you want it to be.

Once you have established some goals that you'd like to accomplish, experiment to see what works and what doesn't. Here are some suggestions of things to experiment with:

1.      Structure. If you have a goal to practice the tuba for an hour every day, do you find that it helps to stick to a schedule and practice at the same time every day? Or do you prefer to be free to practice whenever you feel like it, as long as you get in an hour of practice? If you're not sure, try practicing for one week on a schedule and one week without a schedule, and see which method you prefer, or which one makes you better able to follow your goal.

Experiment also with practicing at different times of day. You may find you're more alert in the evening than in the morning. You may find that practicing feels like a chore if you do it right after work or school, but is fun if you take a break to relax first. Try different things and record how you feel and what works. If you feel attached to the daily routine that you have already, without tuba practice, try to work your goal into the routine where it seems to fit, rather than disrupting your routine.

See whether you work better practicing for shorter or longer increments of time. Is it better for you to practice for one hour straight, or do you prefer two thirty-minute sessions, or three twenty-minute sessions? If you decide to split your practicing into smaller increments, do you just like a short break in the middle of your hour-long practice session? Or do you prefer to do half of your practicing before breakfast and the other half just before bed? Experiment and find what works best.

2.      Environment. What kind of environment do you work best in? Do you prefer complete silence, a little bit of background noise, or a lot of background noise? Do you work better while listening to music or TV? Do you like to work alone or with others? Do you like the presence of other people, such as in a library or coffee shop? Do you like to sit at a desk, recline on the couch, or lie on the grass outside? Try different methods and see what works.

3.      Organized activities. Do you find that being involved in organized activities works better for you than doing something on your own? Some activities naturally require meeting at regular times with a group, such as being in a play, in a band, or on a sports team. But how do you feel when it comes to activities that you *can* do on your own, such as reading, writing, or art? If you want to write more poetry, would you be happy doing it on your own? Or would you enjoy being part of a poetry club that meets regularly? If you are unsure, you could try joining a group and see how you like it.

If you decide to join a group, pay attention to how you like the group and how much progress you are making with you goal once you start. If you never find time to crochet, but meeting with a crocheting club ensures that you'll get to make at least some progress every week, the group is probably working well for you. If you find that the members of a poetry club spend most of the meetings goofing off instead of sharing poetry, but you make a lot of new friends and still have fun at the meetings, you may decide to stay in the club for fun, but also dedicate more time to poetry writing on your own. If you thought art club would be fun, but you find that the people aren't welcoming or you

180

don't fit in, and you find yourself dreading going to the meetings, then it's good to sit down and think about whether you should really stay with the group or not. Remember that there is more than one way to accomplish a goal. If you don't like a particular group, you can try joining another group or working on the goal on your own. No one in the group should make you feel like you have to stay in order to achieve your goals.

4.      Getting others involved. Some people find that having friends involved can be a motivating factor because you can push each other to do things that you wouldn't be motivated to do own your own. If this sounds like you, you may want to find a friend who shares your interest and ask if they'd like to join you. If you do this, pay attention to how having a friend involved affects you. Do you feel more motivated about your goal in a positive way? Or do you not like the added pressure of being accountable to someone else?

Make sure that involving a friend is helping your progress. If your goal is to clean up litter in your neighborhood and you've invited friends to help you, make sure you are getting the work done and not just hanging out.

Try not to automatically assume that everyone who shares your interest will want to work with you. Some people prefer to work alone. If your friend goes jogging every night after dinner, they may love for you to join them, but they might also want that time to themself. When you ask, tell them you'd love to join them, but you will understand if they prefer to jog alone. If they say no, don't push the issue.

If your friend does welcome you to join them, make sure you both understand what kind of motivation you want from each other. The fact that your friend said you could jog with them does not necessarily mean that they want you to push them to go jogging when they don't feel like it, even if you'd like them to do that for you. Discuss ahead of time how much of a push you each want, and accept it if your friend does not want you to push them on days when they don't feel like jogging. Your goals do not have to be the same for you to have a mutually beneficial relationship – it's totally fine if you're in it for the workout and your friend is in it for the chance to spend time with you. But make sure that you are not pushing your own goals on your friend. It's one thing to say, "I love that we can go jogging together – you really motivate me!" But it's another to say, "You have to keep coming jogging because it motivates me!" Pay attention to any signs that your new partnership is putting a strain on your friendship.

5.       Talking about it. Even if you don't want to work with anyone else, some people find it helpful to tell others about their goal. Sharing can add accountability because the friends you tell may check in and see how much you've done.  It is entirely up to you whether you think sharing your goal will be helpful or unhelpful. Think about how you've felt in the past when you shared your goals with others. Have you found it helpful to have friends or family ask about your goal and cheer you on? Have you ever wished you hadn't told someone about a goal because they started nagging you about it? Think about what has worked for you in the past, and choose people who will encourage you while also respecting your boundaries. Be clear about what level of involvement you are requesting.

6.       What effect does time pressure have on you? Do you prefer to set a deadline that will push you to reach your goal sooner, or are you better able to focus when you know you have plenty of time? If your goal is long-term, you can set deadlines for benchmarks you want to reach.

7.       Do you prefer to start with the easier parts or the harder parts? This preference can vary from one activity to the next, so it is worth experimenting.

8.       Do you find it helpful to read about or hear from other people who have achieved what you're working on, or who have achieved great things in general? Or does that make you feel pressured to do things their way or feel inadequate compared to them? What effect do motivational quotes have on you? Try to engage in things that will help you and make you feel good about your goal, and avoid things that will hinder your progress or make you feel bad about your goal.

9.       Are you intrinsically motivated to work on your goal, or do you often feel unmotivated?

If you definitely want to achieve your goal but find yourself unmotivated to work on it, think about what might motivate you. Would it help to visualize yourself achieving your goal? Would it help to make a poster relating to your goal that you can see every day?

Look for ways that you can make the day-to-day work more efficient, convenient, or enjoyable to you. For example, if you want to practice for basketball team tryouts but get tired of practicing alone, see if a friend who likes basketball would like to play one-on-one with you sometimes. If you need to practice drills and can't have a friend over to play basketball every day, you could try challenging some friends to a once-a-week basketball game or hoop-shooting contest. If basketball tryouts are far away, this will give you shorter-term motivation because you can practice every week with the intention of trying to beat your friends when you play together.

Some people will recommend that you offer yourself rewards in order to get things done when you don't feel like doing them. This can be helpful, but external rewards can also interfere with the way you feel about your goals. Pay attention to the effects of rewarding yourself. If you have one week where you promise yourself an ice cream sundae on the weekend if you practice dance every day, try practicing every day the following week without rewarding yourself and see which way makes you feel better.

You may be wondering why anyone would choose not getting an ice cream sundae over getting one, but rewards can be complicated. Motivation can be internal or external. Internal motivation comes from you. It means that you are motivated to do something because you are truly interested in doing it. Even if you don't always feel like practicing dance, you can feel motivated by your internal desire to be a better dancer, and becoming a better dancer will be a reward in and of itself. External motivation means that you are motivated by something unrelated to the task itself, such as doing a job to get paid, or behaving the way you're expected to behave in school to avoid getting in trouble, even if you did not personally want to do the job or behave as you were told. While you may find that rewarding yourself with ice cream makes you more likely to practice dance every day, you could also find that the ice cream actually interferes with your love of dance. I personally have found that doing something for an external reward makes me *less* interested in the activity, because I know that if I really liked an activity, I would do it on my own, without needing a reward. Being offered a reward for doing something tells me that the activity must *not* be something that I truly want to do. I also find that when an external reward is unrelated to the goal itself, the goal can start to feel like an obstacle standing between me and something I would otherwise be able to have (because you *can* have an ice cream sundae without practicing dance), which can cause me to resent the goal. It is important to notice how rewards work for you, not just in terms of how much practicing you get done on a given week, but in terms of whether you are maintaining your interest or passion in what you are doing.

If you find that external rewards are not for you, but you are still looking for some kind of short-term gratification when your dance audition is months away, try rewarding yourself with a chance to use the skills you're developing. Maybe after a certain amount of practice, you can plan to put on a mini dance recital for your family or friends. Because this type of reward is directly related to dance (you would need to practice to perform well in your mini recital), it is likely to maintain your internal motivation, while also giving you more instant gratification than if you just waited until your audition to perform.

# Self-Knowledge and Decision-Making

[Note: The exercises in this section are for the purpose of understanding yourself, and are not intended to make you feel guilty or bad about yourself in any way. However, some of the exercises *could* trigger negative feelings about yourself, so feel free to skip over any exercises that you think might leave you feeling bad.]

Self-validation is also necessary when it comes to making choices. In a culture full of social pressures and invalidation, it can be hard to make the decisions that are right for you. When you feel yourself being pulled in all different directions, this advice may help you to do what is right for you.

## Social Influence Is Pervasive

Even if you make a decision entirely on your own, without discussing it with anybody, you might still be influenced by other people's opinions. We've talked a lot about how to help other people make the choices that are right for them, and how we can inadvertently pressure people to do things that they don't want to do. The same issue exists when we are trying to make our own decisions. Think about when you were younger: If your friends all wanted to do something that you knew your parents would not be happy about, you would probably feel at least slightly uncomfortable going along with it, even if you knew that your parents would never find out. Other people's opinions and influences can stay with us, even when those people aren't around, even if we never discuss the decision with them. Even if you are sitting in bed alone, making a personal list of priorities or pros and cons, you may find yourself including things that don't matter to you and suppressing things that do matter to you in an effort to be more socially desirable. This does not mean that you can't make your own decisions, but it is good to be aware of your external influences so that you can separate your true desires from those influences if you need to. Try these exercises:

Priority List - Make a priority list based on what matters to you, *regardless* of your actual behavior. Maybe you've always put school ahead of volleyball because you were told to, but you know in your heart that volleyball is more important to you. Even if other people (such as your parents) or life circumstances (such as needing money to survive) are controlling your actions, only *you* can decide what you like, what you care about, and the order of your priorities. No one else can tell you how to feel:

_____

_____

_____

_____

Quality List - Close your eyes and pretend that you're *not* at an interview. You're not trying to talk your way into something or convince anyone of anything. List the qualities that you feel describe you:

_____

_____

_____

_____

Read over your list and ask yourself, "Is this a list that I would share with anyone that I need to make a good impression on?" If the answer is yes, then you've most likely left some things out. Go back and add the qualities that you would *never* share with someone you were trying to impress. This does not mean that there is anything wrong with these qualities, it just means that they are qualities that are not valued in your culture. If you ignore some parts of yourself just because your culture doesn't like them, you will end up with an inaccurate idea of who you are and what will make you happy. For instance, if you are introverted but are always presenting yourself as an extrovert, you may start to believe that you really *are* extroverted, and you might put yourself in a situation that involves too much social interaction and not enough personal time. If you never keep your living space clean or organized, but you make an effort to hide that from other people, you could end up with a roommate or partner who is constantly pressuring you to clean when you don't want to, because they assumed that you were neater based on what they saw before they moved in with you. Truly knowing yourself will help you to find the people and situations that are a good fit for you.

Pros and Cons List – When you have to make an important decision and you are making a pros and cons list, make a conscious effort to focus on your own feelings, even if you have different values than your parents, your friends, or your society. After you have listed out all of the pros and cons, think about which factors matter the most to you, and about which factors are essential and non-essential to you.

Sometimes we can be more focused on what we want than on what we already have. If you are unsatisfied with your life and are looking for a major change, then it's totally fine to focus more on what you hope will be different about the new situation. But when you are thinking about what matters to you, it's also good to keep in mind what you have in your current situation that you are not willing to live without. There is an old joke where an older fish asks a younger fish, "How's the water?" and the younger fish replies, "What's water?" It is easy to overlook things that are part of our daily lives, and not stop and think about how we'd feel if we didn't have them. Take the time to observe all of the things you have in your life that are important to you. Writing a list of all these things will be helpful to you when deciding whether or not a new situation will work for you.

After you've made your list of what matters to you, think hard about what you may not have included. Remember, this is *your* list, for your eyes only. Think about things that would matter to you in a new situation such as:

- Feeling good about yourself in a particular environment and not feeling intimidated.
- Having plenty of care and attention.
- Being able to express yourself freely – not having a lot of social pressure about how to dress, what to talk about, or what your interests should be.
- Being able to eat what you want in front of others without feeling pressured to be on any particular kind of diet.
- Not being the only person of your race, religion, or ethnic background in a particular environment.
- Being able to express negative feelings – not having to smile or act cheerful.
- Being able to hold hands and kiss your same-sex partner in public.
- Being able to openly express your gender identity.
- Not having to hide your disability or mental illness from others.
- Having a lot to do.
- Having a lot of free time.
- Not having to spend too much time alone.

- Not having to spend too much time with other people.
- Having control of your environment (noise, light, temperature).
- Getting to continue playing your video games, watching your TV shows, writing your blog, etc.
- Being able to call, email, or otherwise be in contact with people who are not with you as often as you want.

These are just a few examples, but you get the idea. If something matters to you, take it into account when you make a decision.

<u>Know Your Conditions.</u> Look at each quality that you listed about yourself in the qualities exercise, and ask yourself, "Under what circumstances do I normally have this quality, and under what circumstances would I not have this quality?" Maybe you described yourself as "friendly." Are you friendly all the time? What conditions would cause you to not be friendly? When you haven't had enough sleep? When you haven't had enough fun? When you are in a lot of pain? When you are not able to do things that are part of your normal routine? Really think about this issue for all of the qualities that you listed. Think about the conditions that need to be met in order for you to do different things and function on different levels.

<u>Exercise:</u> Go through the traits that you use to describe yourself, and explain the conditions that must be met in order for you to have those traits:

Trait:_____

Conditions that must be met for me to have this trait:

_____

_____

Trait:_____

Conditions that must be met for me to have this trait:

_____

_____

Trait:_____

Conditions that must be met for me to have this trait:

_____

_____

If you normally have all of your needs met, it can be easy to think that you are just, for instance, friendly all the time, under any circumstance. When you are entering a new situation, it's important to stop and think about whether or not your needs will be met and how you might behave differently depending on the circumstances. While you don't need to announce during a job interview that you are only a nice person when you have your five cups of coffee, that's good information for *you* to have in case they tell you that coffee isn't allowed.

Sustainability – Imagine that someone asked you how much weight you could lift. You think back to the time that you helped you grandfather move, and you carried a 100-lb piece of furniture from the moving van into his apartment. You say that you can lift one hundred pounds. Now, imagine that upon hearing this, someone hands you a backpack that weighs one hundred pounds and tells you that you'll have to carry that backpack every day, all day long. This might not be something that you are capable of doing. And even if you can physically do it, it will probably start to wear you down and disrupt your quality of life. Being able to carry a 100-lb piece of furniture a short distance one time does not mean that you could carry a 100-lb backpack all the time. Most of us have been taught that we should present the best of ourselves to people. Especially in cases like interviews, we're told that we *should* think back to the heaviest object we've ever lifted, no matter how short of a time we actually held it. It's important to keep sustainability in mind when you present yourself. When it comes to any trait – how sociable you are, how long you can sit still, etc., think in terms of how much weight could reasonably carry in a backpack all the time, rather than the most you've ever done one time.

## Internal Desire

Maybe you've been raised to think that you're going to marry someone of the opposite sex and have children. Maybe all your friends can't wait to go away to college. Maybe deep down inside, you don't have these desires, but you suppress what you know about yourself because of what you're told you're supposed to want. No matter what other people tell you you're supposed to do, no matter how you've seen something portrayed in the media, and no matter how much your culture values an experience, the desire to do anything has to come from within you. Listen to that nagging feeling that tells you that what you're doing is not such a good idea. If you're confused about what you want, sit down and list the *sources* of your desires. Do you have a personal desire to get away from home, or are you assuming it will be fun because everyone else is looking forward to it? If your friends weren't so excited about it, how would you feel? If your primary source of desire is based on what other people are telling you, ask yourself what you really want. What would you choose if you didn't have anyone influencing you?

Widening/Narrowing Your Range – If you're looking at different choices, people will sometimes tell you to keep all your options open. This is perfectly fine if you *want* to keep all your options open. But you know yourself. If you know that you won't be happy with choices that don't meet certain criteria or are outside of a certain range, then don't feel obligated to consider those choices. There is nothing wrong with having a smaller range of possibilities.

Alternatively, sometimes people will tell you to keep your options within a certain range because they can't imagine that you would be happy with anything else. Maybe you would be happy moving far away, being in a long-distance relationship, taking a job outside of your comfort zone, or having a less stable lifestyle, when other people can't see those things working out for you. You know yourself. If you know that you want to keep a wider range options open, then you should keep them open.

The range of possibilities you consider should be based on how open you truly are to all the choices, not an external pressure to either widen or narrow your range.

Fear/Comfort Zones – We've already discussed that there are times when a person wants to do something that is out of their comfort zone and could use some encouragement, and other times when someone does not want to do something that is out of their comfort zone and does not want to be pushed to do it. The same is true of yourself. Try to find support and encouragement for the things that you do want to try, and keep in mind the things that you don't want to do. People will often treat any out-of-comfort-zone activity as something that you want to be encouraged to do, but you know that there is a difference between wanting to do something and being afraid, and not wanting to do it at all. Don't let people push you into something just to get out of your comfort zone. You know the difference, so trust yourself.

Getting Used to It – We've already discussed that getting used to something does not make it okay, with the example of being new in school (which will get better with time) vs. getting bullied at school (which will not get better with time). Lots of people will tell you that becoming accustomed to something will make the problem go away.

But you know the difference. You know whether or not a problem is just going to disappear over time. If you need to get out of a situation because the problem isn't going away, trust yourself. Don't let people convince you that you will get used to something that you know you are not okay with.

## Telling Yourself the Truth

Think of a class that you did not like, but you were required to take in order graduate from high school. It was probably easy to maintain that you did not enjoy the class. If someone asked you how you liked the class, you could have probably told them that you found it boring. If they asked, "Why are you taking the class then?" you could have replied, "Because it's required," and most likely, the other person would have understood. They would have accepted that graduating was important and would not have questioned your choice any further. And maybe after high school was over, you would never have to take another course in that subject again.

Now, imagine instead that you did an extra-curricular activity in high school that you did not enjoy, either because your parents pushed you to do it, or because your school highly recommended that you have extra-curricular activities to list on your college applications. You didn't really *want* to do the activity, but was not required in the same way that certain classes were required. You also had more choice in the matter because you could have picked a different activity instead. When someone asked you how you liked the activity, you felt awkward saying that you hated it. It was one thing to hate a required class, but it felt silly to say that you hated something that you technically chose to do. If the person asked you, "Why are you doing it if you don't like it?" you would not have had a solid answer. So you said, "It's going well." You said this not just once, but every time that someone asked you about the activity. You even got into discussions about how much you enjoyed this activity with your teachers, your parents' friends, and anyone else who asked. After speaking positively about it for years, you found yourself thinking, "Maybe this activity isn't so bad," even though your interest had not actually changed. Once you were out of high school and could do what you wanted, you found yourself joining this activity again in college or another community setting, only to realize that you were never actually interested.

When you have a strong reason for doing something that you don't want to do, such as needing a class to graduate, it's easier to maintain the fact that you don't want to do it. But when the pressure is more subtle, when your parents or your friends push you to do something that you'd rather not do, you can begin to tell yourself that you actually like something that you don't. This may be harmless if it happens only once, but it can also cause you to make future choices that are not right for you. Expectations that you will get married, have children, go to college, get a certain type of job, etc. can lead you to believe that you want these things when you don't.

Here are some exercises that will help you distinguish what you want from what you don't want:

The Reasons You Do Things. Make a list of some of the things you do, and explain the real reasons that you do them (feel free to add more):

Something I do:_____

Why I do it:_____

Something I do:_____

Why I do it:_____

Something I do:_____

Why I do it:_____

Something I do:_____

Why I do it:_____

Remember, you're not trying to make any kind of impression. No one is seeing this list other than you. Don't be afraid to list reasons like:

- Because all my friends are doing it, and I'd be left out if I weren't doing it too.
- Because I want to get closer to a person I like.
- Because someone pressured me and I didn't feel comfortable saying no.
- Because it pleases my parents or guardians.
- Because it makes me more popular.
- Because it makes a good impression on my employer.
- Because I need to stay on good terms with certain people or else my life will be a nightmare.
- Because I need to do it to survive.
- Because it's easier than trying to find an alternative.

It is important to acknowledge reasons like these to yourself. Again, you do not need to share this with anyone else. This is not about feeling guilty for anything. The purpose of this exercise is to understand what you really like and don't like. You certainly don't need to tell your employer that you hate working with kids and you only got a job at a day camp because your crush works there as well, but this is good information for *you* to keep in mind before you decide to work there again next summer, when your crush is gone.

Reasons You Don't Do Things. This is a reverse of the exercise above. Make a list of the things that you have an interest in but have not yet tried, or don't do very often, and explain why you have not done them or do not do them very often. (Feel free to add more):

Something I like:_____

Why I don't do it:_____

Something I like:_____

Why I don't do it:_____

Something I like:_____

Why I don't do it:_____

Again, this exercise is not to make you feel guilty for not doing things; it is to help you discover things that you would really like to do but haven't tried yet. Maybe you would love to do more of something but have not had the opportunity. If you are thinking of moving to a new city, for instance, the fact that you wish you could do more hiking might influence where you would like to live. Make sure you consider new things you'd like to try, as well as the things that you already know you enjoy.

Know When You're Stretching the Truth. We can't always avoid lying or omitting information to other people. If you hate your job, for instance, you may not want to share that information with your employer until you have another job lined up and are prepared to leave. But if you keep telling everyone that your job is perfectly fine, you may start to believe that yourself and have a harder time bringing yourself to quit. The very act of saying, "Yes, school/work/my relationship is going well," can make you start to believe that these things are actually going well when they are not.

Imagine a balance scale, where evidence that you want to stay at your job is on one side and evidence that you do not want to stay at your job is on the other side. Ideally, all of this evidence would be based on reality – a warm and friendly interaction with your coworker would be evidence that you want to stay, and a hostile interaction with a customer would be evidence that you want to leave. But sometimes, the evidence that goes onto that balance scale is not based on your own experience. The fact that you told someone that you like your job can become evidence that you want to stay, even if you were not telling the truth. Even when you can't tell the truth, you can take some steps to avoid having the lie interfere with your personal beliefs:

1.      Keep it brief. If someone asks how your job is going and you do not want to tell them that you hate it, don't get into a long, detailed discussion about your job where you will have to keep lying about how much you love it. Keep your response brief and change the subject: "My job's going fine. Can you believe how much snow we're supposed to get tomorrow?"

2.      Take a moment to remind yourself of why you are saying something that is not true – you don't want your family to pressure you to stay at your job, you don't want to get let go before you have a new job lined up, you just don't feel like discussing it at the moment, etc. This is not about feeling guilty for lying; it's about reminding yourself that you have a *reason* for lying, which gives more weight to the truth.

3.      If you are regularly telling people that your job is going well when it is not, make sure you regularly remind yourself of how you actually feel. If you have a supportive friend, talk to them about wanting to quit your job. Even if you don't feel like getting into a long discussion about it, just sharing the information that you hate your job with someone else can reiterate that truth to yourself. If you start to tell yourself that maybe your job isn't so bad, you have a friend who can remind you of what you said before and ask why you changed your mind. If you don't have a safe person to share with, you can write your feelings down in a journal, blog, or anyplace else where your employer will not see it. This will also give more weight to the truth in your mind.

## More Tips on Decision-Making

Involving Others – Making the choice that's right for you does not mean you can't consider anyone else's opinion. Other people can be a great source of information. It can be helpful to talk to a mentor, or someone who has experience with the goals that you would like to achieve. If you want to be a teacher, for example, it would be helpful to talk to a teacher about their career path and any advice that they wish they had known when they were first starting out. They can also give you more information about what their job entails and help you figure out whether teaching would be a good fit for you. In addition to people with experience, it can also be helpful to seek advice from people who know you well and respect your goals. Since they are not in the middle of the situation, they may spot issues that you didn't notice. We have talked about the fact that when someone asks you for directions, you need to understand where they want to go before you can help them. The same is true when you are seeking help from someone else. When considering other people's advice, make sure that they understand where you are trying to go.

Get the Facts – It's great to talk to someone who has experience with something you'd like to do, but when you are using someone else's input to help you make a decision, it's important to separate facts from opinions. When someone is describing their experience to you, pay attention to the facts that they share. If someone is telling you how much they love their job, ask them *what* they love about it specifically. If someone says that their city is great because there are lots of cool things to do, ask them what *kinds* of cool things they are talking about. Remember that the person you are talking to is describing their own experience, and the fact that they love or hate something does not necessarily mean that you will feel the same way.

When someone gives you an opinion, don't be afraid to ask for the facts:

If someone says, "Noise has never been an issue for me in this apartment building."

Ask: "How much outside noise can you normally hear from the inside of your apartment, regardless of whether it bothers you?"

If someone says: "This class is not as hard as everyone makes it out to be."

Ask: "How many pages of reading/problem sets do you normally get assigned each week?"

If someone says, "We have a good work-to-life balance at our company."

Ask: "What is your vacation policy?" or "Will overtime work be expected?"

Try to get the most objective information that you can before making a decision.

Correlation Is Not Causation – The fact that everyone in a particular place seems to be happy does not necessarily mean that the place is so awesome that it is *causing* everyone to be happy. It could be that the place tends to attract people who have good lives already. It could be that people who don't like it are quick to leave, leaving the place with only the people who are happiest to be there. It could be that the place is good at only attracting and selecting people who are perfectly suited for that environment. It could also be that people feel the need to present a happy persona in that environment.

It is definitely possible that the place is wonderful and makes everyone happy, but it's always worth a second glance at what's really going on. If you do find that the place itself is great and makes people happy, look at *whom* it is making happy and ask yourself, "Would this make *me* happy?" If a movie theater only shows horror films for years, and over time, only horror fans go to that theater, it will look to an outsider like the theater is doing great and everyone who goes is happy with it, but that doesn't mean that a non-horror fan would like it.

Social Rules Matter – Imagine that a particular school or company does not have a dress code. You read this information and are glad that you have the freedom to wear whatever you want. But when you arrive on your first day, every single person is wearing jeans and a school or company t-shirt. You are the only person wearing something different, and everyone is staring at you all day long. Several people inform you of where you can buy a t-shirt like theirs, without asking you if you want one. Technically speaking, there is no dress code. You won't get in trouble for not dressing like your peers. But would you honestly feel comfortable wearing whatever you wanted in that environment?

Social rules are just as important – and often more important – than official rules. It's not enough to just know what is *allowed* in a certain environment; you need to find out what is *accepted*. It helps if you can explore the environment, observe how people behave, and talk to people who are there about what is socially acceptable and unacceptable.

People Are Promotional. We already talked about not giving sales pitches and instead trying to help friends figure out what will make them happy. But the fact is, people often *do* give sales pitches, and it's important to notice when someone is trying to sell you on an experience because they loved it so much. If it feels like a friend is in sales-pitch mode, try to focus on the facts that they are sharing, and make an informed decision based on what will be best for you.

Understand Cultural Biases. Every culture has its values, which influence people's opinions. When you ask for advice on a decision that you need to make, most of the suggestions you'll get will be based on what is valued in your culture. Keep this in mind when you review peoples' advice to you. Even if everyone you talk to gives the same advice, that advice is not necessarily right for you – it could just be a reflection of cultural values.

Your Past, Present, and Future. We've already talked about the fact that you cannot necessarily predict how younger people will feel about things in the future, because their experience might be different than yours. The same is true when it comes to people saying that they know how you'll feel, what you'll be happy about, and what you'll regret later on. Those people are not you, and your experience might be different from theirs.

Exercise: Make a list of things you've done in the past that you're glad you did, and explain why you're glad that you did them. (These can be things that still affect your life now, or things that only mattered at the time):

Something I did:_____

Why I'm glad I did it:_____

Something I did:_____

Why I'm glad I did it:_____

Something I did:_____

Why I'm glad I did it:_____

Now, make a list of things you've done in the past that you regret, and explain why you regret those things. (These can be things that still affect your life now, or things that only mattered at the time):

Something I did:_____

Why I regret it:_____

Something I did:_____

Why I regret it:_____

Something I did:_____

Why I regret it:_____

Now, look over your reasons and see if you notice any similarities among the kinds of things you're glad you did and the kinds of things you regret. These patterns are likely to be true in the future.

If you know what matters to you and if you know how you feel about what you have already done, you can probably predict how you'll feel in the future about what you're doing now. No one else's experience will be exactly like yours. You know yourself better than anyone else – your past, your present, and yes, even your future.

Understanding yourself does not mean that every decision you make will be right for you. The way to develop self-understanding is to learn from your mistakes, to ask yourself, "Why did I think that this would be good for me, when it wasn't?" "Was this a total surprise, or did I ignore warning signs that this was a bad idea?" "Did I learn anything new about myself that I should take into account in future decisions?" Self-understanding may take time, but it will help lead you to where you want to be.

## But What about the Things You Can't Change?

It's common to get invalidated when you complain about things that people consider to be just a part of life, things that people think you just have to accept. But the fact is, people don't have to just accept things the way they are. Most things don't *need* to be the way they are. Most things *can* be changed, even if we've always been taught that they can't.

Look at these two statements:

1. I need to practice drawing in order to improve my drawing skills.
2. I need to finish my homework in order to play outside.

The first statement has a clear cause-and-effect relationship: You cannot improve your drawing skills without drawing.

But look closely at the second statement. Doing your homework and playing outside are not directly related to each other the way that practicing a skill is related to becoming better at the skill. You are not *incapable* of going outside to play without having finished your homework. If you "need" to do your homework in order to play outside, it is because someone else is forcing you to do it, or because you live in a society where those are the rules.

When you think about it, most of the things that we all "need" to do are more like the homework example than the drawing example. Most of the things we need to do exist because of what other people have told us we have to do, or because of the way our society is constructed. Let's look at some more examples:

"I need to clean my apartment before I invite people over."

Unless your clutter is literally blocking the door so that people can't enter, you do not need to do this. You may *want* to clean your apartment because you like it that way, which is fine, but the fact that you feel the *need* to clean your apartment to have people over even if you don't feel like it – that is something you've been taught. It's a social rule that you're being expected to live by. You didn't have to be taught that cleaning your place was essential to having guests over. You could have been taught that you can keep your space however you like, and that you should be accepting of other people keeping their space the way they like it. The culture does not have to expect you to clean your apartment when you have company.

199

"I need to shave my legs before I can wear shorts."

If you *want* to shave your legs because you personally prefer that look, that is totally fine. But if you are dragging yourself to shave your legs because you don't feel allowed to wear shorts without shaving, that is the product of your society. You didn't have to be taught that there was anything wrong with the hair on your legs, and your culture does not have to say that your natural body hair is not attractive and that you are expected to remove it.

"I need to finish my homework before I can play outside/use my phone/hang out with my friends."

This is a product of our society. We *could* have a society where children and teenagers had more of a say in their own education and how they want to spend their time. We could all create a culture where radical unschooling was normal and acceptable, and adults respected children's choices.

"I need to work to earn money and support myself and my family."

While this statement is certainly true in our current culture, we *could* have an unconditional basic income, which would provide everyone with the money that they need to survive, so that working would be a choice.

Most things that we think of as "just the way things are" are products of our culture and our society that do not need to be the way they are. We have all been taught that we have to just live with certain things, but most of these things, we could actually change. The path to change is not necessarily easy, but it does exist, and it is perfectly legitimate for people to not be okay with things as they are. If you don't have a personal problem with something, if you have long accepted that you need to finish your homework before going outside and you don't wish to spend your time and energy fighting against it, that is fine. But understand that not everyone is okay with every part of our culture, and that you can still validate people's feelings when they express what they are not okay with and support their work to change it.

# Part 5: Redefining Positive

# Painkillers

It might be tempting to offer someone a quick fix when they are upset, something that will make them feel better temporarily until their bad mood passes. But sometimes, small bursts of positivity can actually mask serious issues that a person needs to examine in order to be happy in the long run. If you've ever sprained your ankle, you know how much it hurts to try to walk on it. While you might take medicine to relieve the pain, that initial pain that you feel right when you hurt yourself lets you know that something is wrong. It gets you to stay off of your sprained ankle until it heals. Pain serves an important function – it tells us to stop doing what we're doing so that we don't hurt ourselves further. It tells us that something needs to be fixed.

The same is true for emotional pain. Emotional pain tells us that something is wrong. Sometimes, when someone is feeling bad, the solution is to do an activity that will make them happy. But there are other times when the problem is more serious. If you push someone to distract themself with positive activities when they really want to talk about negative things, it can hinder them from thinking through what's wrong. That can prevent them from getting out of their bad situation or finding a way to fix the problem.

It's not just about problem-solving either. Some people *want* to talk about negative experiences and have those negative experiences validated, and there is no option of them feeling better until the negative things have been validated. When I was having a bad time in college, I got lots of advice for things I could do to make myself feel better – getting more exercise, going outside every day, meditating, etc. The reason these things didn't work was that they didn't satisfy my need to have my bad feelings validated, and they did not help to fix the situation that was causing a problem in the first place. Exercising, being outside, and meditating are all things that could make a person feel better, and they are all things that might be worth recommending if someone is just feeling temporarily down for no apparent reason. But in my case, there *was* an apparent reason. I missed my parents, my home, and having lots of time to myself, and a rush of endorphin or fresh air can't fix those problems any more than cough syrup can cure strep throat. All the suggested remedies that I got in college – even those coming from counselors – were just painkillers. All the temporary relief I got in college made me numb to how big the problem was. I was a senior by the time I realized that I should have listened to my gut and left the school after my first semester. Now, if a person doesn't *want* to think about the negative situation and they prefer to have positive distractions, that is totally fine. Don't push someone to talk about a difficult situation if they don't want to. But if they *do* want to talk about something negative, even for a very long time, *listen.* Don't try to persuade them to think more positively. It may be talking to you that helps someone to work out their feelings and realize that they want to get out of a situation that is not working for them. They might never discover that if they are always pushed to be more positive.

# How to Be "Awesome"

One of my college dorms had a bulletin board with topics such as "Ways to Go Green," or "What Diversity Means to Me," and the resident advisor would post ideas for everyone to read. One time, the topic was "How to Be Awesome." The board was full of messages such as "Smile more!" "Be optimistic!" "Leave the past behind you!" "Just shower every day – it's not that hard!" "Stop complaining so much!" "Making these simple changes will make you more likable!" and other messages that pushed people to be positive. My friend Eli pinned a note to the board saying that these responses were problematic, and another student responded with a note that said, "It doesn't explicitly target you." Eli typed up this response and posted it to the board:

*It does explicitly target me. I'd like to be able to say that the ableism here is something subtle, something hard to recognize, something easily forgivable. It's not. It's very, very explicit.*

*How does this board target me specifically? It attacks people who don't shower every day. I am such a person. First of all, showering every day is not very healthy for your skin; if I do shower each day for several days in a row, my skin gets somewhat dried-out and feels bad. But moreover, I am very sensitive to physical touch – presumably as a result of my having Asperger's Syndrome. (For the same reason, I have trouble writing with a pencil for significant amounts of time, hence why I've typed this response instead of writing it out). This board naively says that it's "not that hard" to shower once a day. It is hard for me, and I'm sure I'm far from the only one.*

*The "humorous" statements here completely erase my experiences, the experiences of my friends who have battled depression, the experiences of anyone with a mental or physical ability that keeps them from presenting the happy, confident, on-top-of-the-world persona presented here. When it says "It is impossible to be awesome if you do not have the learning ability to back it up," that is an overt attack against people with learning disabilities. When it says "The past is old news, so there is no reason to let it affect your future," that is an overt attack against people who are deeply affected by their pasts.*

205

*But those things are merely details. Taking a step back, the entire message of the board is at fault. I don't appreciate being told to be happy in a world that has done little to inspire my happiness. I don't appreciate being told that my worth is based on how much I am liked by other people. I don't appreciate being told that "awesomeness" is determined by these mundane, superficial attributes rather than my skills and passions.*

*Most of all, I don't appreciate this active encouragement of an environment where people hide their troubles and put on a façade of confidence and happiness. All of us have problems in our lives, and these problems need to be addressed, not ignored; discussed, not hidden. What are friends for if not to help us when we are weak? Anyone who is less "likely to hang with" me because I am open about what affects me is not a person who I want to be hanging with at all.*

*I am Eli Dupree, and I am awesome, despite what this bulletin board says. I'd be happy to talk to you (or anyone else) in person about this; I live in [dorm room number], and my door is always open. (Don't worry, I'm a lot more friendly than I sound in a text-based argument! I have strong opinions about this issue, but I bear no hostility towards you as a person, and always love to exchange points of view).*

*-Eli Dupree*[1]

---

[1] If you want to read more of Eli's writing, you can visit their website at elidupree.com.

# The Trouble with Positive Thinking

There is a lot of pressure to be positive and smiling all the time, but the truth is that pushing people to be positive when they are not feeling that way is invalidating, and can often have a negative effect on people's lives.

Observe this conversation:

Tameka: "I hated that party."

Katie: "You didn't have any fun at all?"

Tameka: "Not really."

Katie: "But there must have been something you liked?"

Tameka: "No. It just wasn't my kind of party."

Katie: "But what about when we played games?"

Tameka: "No, I wasn't into the games we played."

Katie: "How about when we all danced?"

Tameka: "I don't really like dancing."

Katie: "But, um…there was root beer at the party! You like root beer, right?"

Tameka: "Yeah..."

Katie: "So you did have some fun at the party!"

Tameka: "Um, yeah, I guess…"

Now, do you think that after talking with Katie, Tameka actually reached the conclusion that the party was lots of fun? Or does it look like the party really wasn't any fun for Tameka and Katie is the one who's not accepting it? Conversations like this are all too common. I've seen a lot of people pressure others into finding some joy in every single thing and being happy and positive all the time. But the truth is, is perfectly okay to not enjoy every single experience you have. And it's okay for other people to have experiences that they don't enjoy. If someone says they didn't have any fun at a party, *that's okay*. It's okay if you had fun at a party and someone else did not.

Accepting that someone had a negative experience can be especially difficult if you felt at all responsible for their experience. If you were hosting the party in question, you may have felt responsible for everyone having a good time. Even if you weren't hosting the party, you might have felt an obligation to make sure that your friend had fun. When your friend tells you that they didn't have fun, you may feel guilty, either because you felt a responsibility to them, or because you were having fun right beside them and didn't realize that anything was

207

wrong. You may feel like you should have done something to make their experience better. You may find yourself denying your friend's experience as a way to escape the guilt. It would make *you* feel a lot more comfortable if your friend had fun. While feeling a certain level of responsibility to your friends is a good thing, don't let this guilt deny your friends the right to their own feelings. Things to remember:

1.      Everything is not for everyone. If your friends did not enjoy something that you did, it could just be a matter of different interests or personality differences, and there is nothing that you could have done to make this particular experience a good one for your friend. If your friend feels like talking about it, ask them in a non-accusatory way why they didn't like the party, and talk to them about what they like and don't like so that you can learn more about their preferences for the future.

2.      Everyone *can't* participate in everything. Your friend could have physical limitations, sensory issues, mental health issues, or a number of other differences that could prevent them from participating in the party. For instance, maybe there were strobe lights at the party and strobe lights cause your friend to have seizures, so they had to sit in a different room by themself all night. When you are able to participate in everything without a problem, you don't always notice the ways in which a situation can be non-inclusive to people who have issues that you do not have.

3.      Remember that there is always room for improvement. If there is something you could have done to make the experience better for your friend and you didn't do it, that does not make you a bad person – it means that you can improve next time. Ask your friend if there is anything you could have done to make the party better for them, listen closely, and learn what you can do going forward.

4.      If you really messed up – for instance, you invited your friend to your strobe light dance party when they have already told you that strobe lights are a problem for them, you didn't tell them ahead of time that there would be strobe lights, and you were not willing to turn the strobe lights off because everyone else was having fun – apologize sincerely to your friend, let them know that you understand what you did wrong, and that you will not do it again. Everyone makes mistakes, and the first step to making things right with your friend is to accept how you made your friend feel. In a case like this, it can be very tempting to convince your friend that the party really was fun and it was their own fault that

they didn't have a good time. Don't do it. Let your friend be upset. Don't try to erase that experience.

Denying someone's negative experience can cause a lot of problems. Refer back to the conversation about the party, when Tameka says, "Um, yeah, I guess…" Now, Tameka may know perfectly well that the party was not fun for her, and she's just saying "Yeah, I guess" because she doesn't know what else to say. But it's also possible that through Katie's persuasion, Tameka has begun to doubt whether her experience was actually as bad as it was. This is not a good thing. If after Katie reminded her about some of the fun events at the party, Tameka decided *on her own* that it actually was a fun party and she will look back on it as a positive memory, that's fine. But if Tameka truly feels like the party was not fun and the only reason she is changing her opinion is because Katie is influencing her, Katie is denying Tameka's experience, and as a result Tameka is lying to herself. By lying to herself about this party, Tameka loses the chance to develop self-knowledge, to learn about her own likes and dislikes, and to remember this party for what it was when she thinks about going to other similar parties in the future. Tameka may learn that she is *supposed* to like parties such as this, and push herself to go to more when she would be much happier doing other things with her time. Tameka is more likely to end up in *more* scenarios that she doesn't like if her experience of not liking this party is denied.

Now, let's change the party scenario a little bit:
Tameka: "I didn't have any fun at that party! When we played truth or dare, Hailey asked me who I had a crush on, and everyone laughed at me for liking another girl and made fun of me for the rest of the party. It was totally humiliating! I thought I could trust all of you to accept me!"
Katie: "Come on, you know we were only joking around, right?"
Tameka: "Um, yeah I guess…"

See what happened here? Katie and her friends were disrespectful to Tameka at this party, and Tameka learned something about all of them from this experience. But if Katie manages to assure Tameka that nothing was wrong, Tameka may internally deny the fact that she doesn't feel she can trust these friends, and she may put herself in a position where they can hurt her again. Tameka *needs* to acknowledge how bad she felt at the party in order to either discuss the issue with the group and work it out, or walk away or distance herself from them. If Tameka is pressured into thinking positively about this party, she is likely to be hurt again and again.

When you push someone to like something they don't like or to think positively about something that is not positive for them, you are denying their experience. This can lead the person to internalize the idea that they actually did enjoy something that they didn't, or the idea that it is not okay for them to feel the way that they felt.

Sometimes we place so much emphasis on finding happiness that we forget that it's okay to have other feelings too. It's okay to hate things! It really is! You don't have to like everything. You don't have to find good in everything. It is perfectly okay to say, "You know what? That was a horrible experience, I wish I hadn't done it, and I never want to do it again!" There is nothing at all wrong with that. In fact, thinking like this can even help you to make choices that will make you happier in the future. Now, if someone tells you that they're upset *about* something being a total washout, meaning that they wish they could find something good to take away from the situation, then it would be perfectly fine to help them come up with a silver lining. But if the person is upset *because* something was a total washout, and they are very clear about the fact that it *was* a washout, *accept their feelings.* Everyone does not want to derive something good out of everything, and you are erasing their experience if you try to convince them that there should be something positive to take away from it when they tell you that there is not. If you want to find the positive in your own bad circumstances and have no regrets, that's fine, but accept that other people do have regrets, and that's okay.

## Positive Attitudes Don't Always Work

Having a positive attitude or positive outlook on things does not work for everyone, and it can actually cause problems. You may have heard people say that if you go into an experience with the attitude it's going to be great, it will be great, and if you go into it with the attitude that it's going to be terrible, it will be terrible – it's all about your attitude. This is not true. Some people find that they enjoy an event more if they assume that it's going to be great from the start. But this is not the only way to do things. There are benefits to approaching something with a negative or cautious attitude – that you don't think things are going to go well and that you need to be on guard or prepared for the worst. There are also benefits to approaching something with a more neutral attitude, not assuming that things will go one way or another. Here's a true story of how my "positive attitude" got me into a mess:

I've already talked about other people denying my experiences in college. But the truth is that, in the early stages of college, I denied a lot of my own experiences. If I had ever sat down and just focused on how I felt, I would have said at any given moment, on any given day, that I was miserable and I wanted to go home. But these immediate feelings were not at the forefront of my mind. At the forefront of my mind was the idea that college would be the best four years of my life. At the forefront of my mind was the fact that everyone at home expected me to thrive in college and to have the time of my life there. At the forefront of my mind was the fact that every person around me acted like our college was the best thing that had ever happened to them. As scared as I was about going away to college, I went into it with a positive outlook. Whenever a worry crossed my mind, like wondering how much I would miss home or if I would be okay living in a dorm, I didn't think through what I would actually do if these problems arose. I didn't voice all of my serious concerns. I pushed them to the back of my mind. I just kept telling myself that everything would be okay, that I should have a positive attitude and look forward to college because everyone around me was looking forward to it, because I was the kind of person who would thrive in college and because college is the best four years of your life. When I look back on it now, I know that if I had actually processed all of my negative feelings about college, if I had expressed every concern that was really on my mind, if I had been honest with myself and others about what I was okay and not okay with, and if I did not

211

have a competing force in my brain that told me, "Everything is going to be all right," I would have realized, both from listening to myself and from discussing it with others, that going far away from home to a "prestigious" college was not the right choice for me.

Remember that story I mentioned in the "No Comparison" chapter, when my friend was visiting her brother at his college, he had a medical emergency, and no one in the dorm would help? I got that phone call during a time when I was seriously questioning whether I wanted to be at my college or not. I was conflicted between my true feelings and the feelings that I thought I was supposed to have about my school. When I heard the story of how everyone at my friend's brother's college was unresponsive, I realized that the students at my school would never behave that way. If I had had a physical medical emergency, I know that any students I ran into at my college would have helped me. Even though I was miserable at my college, I latched onto this idea that it must not be so bad because my friend's brother's school was worse. People often use comparisons to invalidate other people's feelings, by saying, "You shouldn't feel so bad because other people have it worse." Because of this, people learn to use comparisons to invalidate their own experiences, too. This feeling inside myself was detrimental to me – it inhibited me from making the right decision which would have been to leave my college. It was because of positive thinking and denial of what was really going on that I stayed in such a mess for four years.

## Stop Victim-Blaming

[Content: reference to abuse and sexual assault]

When I was a child, we grew up with the story of *The Three Little Pigs* and learned that it was our own responsibility to build strong houses. We learned that if a person doesn't have a home held together with bricks and cement, it is their own fault if a wolf comes along, blows their house down, and eats them alive. But a wolf is not a hurricane that can't be stopped. The wolf in the story has just as much control over his actions as the three little pigs do. The wolf is perfectly capable of walking past the houses made of straw and sticks without blowing them down. Yet, when we tell the story, we don't assign that responsibility to the wolf. We blame the victims for something that was not their fault or their responsibility. Like the wolf, *we* all have agency as well. We can choose not blow people's houses down.

When we think of a person who is positive, we often think of someone who is optimistic, who focuses on the positive aspects of their life, and who smiles even when things go wrong. We think about someone who has a metaphorical brick house and a sturdy roof over their head, so that they *can* still have fun and be happy during a freezing rain storm that has other people ducking under trees for cover. Everyone isn't made out of bricks and stone. Everyone doesn't have the resources and support system to form a sturdy house around themselves that can withstand the elements. Being a positive force in someone's life means understanding that everyone doesn't have the same kind of house that you do, that some houses are made of materials like straw or sticks because those are the only materials that the people had to work with, and that some people don't have houses at all. It means not treating everyone like they can simply build a brick house no matter what else is going on.

If someone can build a strong house and keep out a harmful force, that's great. But if we focus on holding people responsible for their houses, rather than focusing on getting rid of the harmful force in the first place, that's a form of victim-blaming. And the truth is, our positive-attitude culture has victim-blaming embedded in it. We tell people that life is 10% what happens and 90% how you react to it, and that people are products of their choices rather than their circumstances, but these statements are not true and they flat-out blame people for their own troubles, which, in most cases, are not their fault:

-You don't choose your family.

-You don't choose how much money your family has.

-You don't choose to live in a world where people attack you just because of your race.

    -Or who you're attracted to.

    -Or your size.

    -Or your gender identity.

-You don't choose to have a disability.

-You don't choose to have a physical or mental illness.

-You don't choose to live in a world where most people won't accommodate your differences and make it easier for you to function.

-You don't choose to be required to go to school.

-You don't choose to get bullied.

-You don't choose to get raped.

-You don't choose to be abused.

-You don't choose to need to make money to survive.

If we had a world where everyone *truly* had all of the same opportunities to do what would make them happy, meaning that every option was accessible to everyone, both financially and in terms of people's abilities, that no one was forced to do things that they just weren't suited for, and nobody was bullied, abused, or otherwise purposely hurt by other people, then it may be accurate to say that people in this world would be products of their choices, more so than their circumstances. But this is nowhere near the world that we live in.

It's easy to say that people are just positive or negative. It's easy to think that some people will just never be happy no matter what circumstances they're in. Think of someone whom you consider to just be a negative person. Then ask yourself: Have you ever seen them in the situation just described? Have you ever seen them have the freedom to be completely in their own element, with a strong support system of people who accept and love them for who they are, without having to worry about paying bills, or keeping up their grades, or other people hurting them?

When we blame other people for their own unhappiness, it removes *our* responsibility. If you were hosting a party and found out that one of your guests had a miserable time, you'd probably feel guilty because you would feel some level of responsibility to them. But if someone else told you, "Oh, he's just always in a bad mood, he never likes anything," then you'd probably feel better. You'd feel like it wasn't your fault and there was nothing you could have done. When you brush someone off as just being negative all the time, you remove any kind of responsibility you might have had to treat them better. Imagine that someone punched you in the face and broke your nose, and then said, "It's not my problem! You *let* me punch you in the face. You *let* your nose get broken. Why don't you have a stronger nose? Why don't you have better reflexes to get out of my way when I feel like punching? It's certainly not *my* problem that your face happened to be where my fist was!" This is how we talk to each other in a lot of situations, when we blame people for things that were not their fault. Even if you are not the one who actually hurt the person, there might be something that you can do to make their situation better, even if it just means listening, believing them about the problem, and supporting them. There might be ways for you to help improve the culture so that it will no longer be acceptable for the bad thing to happen.

When we tell everyone that their happiness and well-being is their own responsibility, we prevent anything from changing to make life better for people. If a school had a rule that students could only bring peanut butter sandwiches for lunch, most people would recognize that this would be a problem for students with peanut allergies. But once you place the responsibility on the individuals, once you start saying, "Allergies are a myth, you can learn to tolerate anything, but you're just not trying hard enough," then it becomes the students who are at fault, rather than the school. And the students with allergies will suffer for it if no one believes that it's not their fault, it's the system that needs to change.

When I was younger, I used to have stickers on my bedrooms walls that said things like "I'm not afraid to be different," and "Being real is easier than being fake." While these are positive sentiments, they are not enough. The truth is that being real is not always easier than being fake: people get discriminated against, bullied, harassed, punished, fired, disowned, kicked out of their homes, and even murdered for being themselves. It is not enough to tell people to just work harder, smile more, think positive thoughts, or to just get out there and be their awesome selves. We need to make it so that people are *able* to be themselves. Don't just tell someone, "Be yourself!" – *show* them that they can be their true self with you.

## Don't Be a Fair-Weather Friend

Imagine that you and your friends are very physically active – most of your time together is spent playing sports and doing physically strenuous activities. Then one day, you are in a car accident and suffer a serious injury, making you unable to participate in strenuous activities the way that you used to. You hope that your friends will be supportive and accommodate your needs, but instead, they stop inviting you to do things with them. Whenever you are around, they act like it's such a pain in the neck to have to deal with you since you can't physically keep up with them anymore, and they gradually cut you out of their lives so that you'll no longer be slowing them down. How would this make you feel? Would these people be acting like good friends? Would you consider them to be positive forces in your life?

Some people say that you should surround yourself with "positive people" and eliminate "negative people" from your life. But if you do, you are acting exactly like the friends in the scenario above. Everyone does not have a happy life. This advice only encourages people to avoid having friends who are unhappy or who are going through a difficult time, which further isolates people who need friends the most. It encourages people to let go of friends who used to be fun to be around, but are no longer in good spirits because of circumstances that they are going through. When we act like this, we all become fair-weather friends, and when too many of our friends are fair-weather friends, we are forced to pretend that we feel better than we actually do, for fear that we will be abandoned if we are honest about our feelings. True friends do not limit their social circles to only positive people. You may be a positive, fun person to be around right now, but something can happen in your life that will make you feel bad and stop being happy and positive all the time. You don't want people in your life who only want to be around you when you are positive and who will leave you when you stop being happy. And you don't want to *be* that kind of friend either.

If you want to eliminate negativity in your life, don't judge people for whether or not they are in a positive mood most of the time – think about whether or not they are positive *forces* in your life. Positive people can be positive forces in your life, but they can also be negative forces. Negative people can be negative forces in your life, but they can also be positive forces. If someone is always smiling, is lots of

216

fun to be around, and is very satisfied with their own life, you cannot conclude that they would be supportive of you during a difficult time. If someone never smiles, is usually in a more serious mood, and does not have a happy life, you cannot conclude that they would not be a good friend to you if you needed them. There is not always a correlation between whether someone is a happy, positive person, and whether they are a true friend through thick and thin.

Do you want to know who the positive forces are in your life? Think about who was there for you when you were in the hospital, when you got dumped, or when you got kicked out of your home. Who made the difficult times in your life less difficult, whether by taking you out to have fun, by letting you rant to them for hours on end, or by helping you when you needed it the most? Who did you feel that you could be yourself around, that you never had to pretend to be happier, more functional, or more emotionally stable than you actually were? Referring back to your answers in the "Most Important Conversation to Have" chapter, who gives you the kind of support that you need? *These people are the positive forces in your life.* If you validate other people's feelings and give them the kind of support that they need, you will be a positive force in theirs.

# The Real World

Everyone will tell you that you need to accept the unacceptable in order to survive in the real world, but what they often neglect to tell you is that you are *part* of the real world. There is no need to prepare for a real world that you don't like – you can change the real world to match what you want it to be. If a teacher says something like, "If you think I'm too tough, just wait until you have a boss!" you can decide that you are *not* going to be tough like this person when you become a teacher, boss, or whatever you want to be. You can decide that you're going to be the kind of person that you would *want* to run into in the "real world." And you don't need to have an official position of power to do it. If, when you were going through a difficult time, no one helped you and people told you to suck it up or get over it, you can decide that when someone else is going through a difficult time, you will validate their feelings and treat them with compassion. You can make the world a place where people don't have to act okay when they're not. You can make it so that anyone who told you that you needed to toughen up for the real world was wrong, because you are making your part of the real world a place where other people don't have to toughen up. When you think about all the horrible things that have happened in history, and that are happening now, remember that people thought those things were okay, just a part of life, just part of the real world. But many things are better now, and it's all because of people who didn't accept the real world as it was. Every change that has ever happened, and every change that will ever happen begins with someone standing up and saying, "I'm not okay with that." So, say what you're not okay with, validate those who speak out about what they're not okay with, and you will be a true positive force in the world.

# Appendix

## Validation Checklist

_____When someone expresses their feelings about something, I accept their feelings at face value, even if I would never feel the same way about the same thing. I do not accuse anyone of "overreacting" when they have a stronger reaction than I would have expected.

_____I understand that we are all different, that some things that make me happy would make others miserable, and some things that make me miserable would make others happy.

_____I do not tell anyone to suck it up, tough it out, get over it, grow up, or anything else that pushes them to accept things that they are not okay with.

_____If I have a problem with a person's behavior towards myself or others, I speak to them specifically about their behavior. I do not criticize or invalidate the feelings that led them to behave that way.

_____If I do not have the energy to listen to someone complaining or to help them, I tell them how I'm feeling in a way that does not put them down for how they are feeling.

_____I do not cut down people's complaints by telling them that there are bigger problems in the world. I do not purposely use my own problems, or anyone else's, to one-up someone when they are complaining.

_____I understand that people younger than me might have problems that I did not have at their age, or that most people would not have complained about or taken seriously when I was their age, and that those problems are still real and valid.

_____I understand that people may still be affected by things that happened a long time ago. I do not expect anyone to be "over" something just because time has passed.

_____I validate the feelings of people who experience forms of oppression that I don't. What people tell me about their experience of oppression is real, even if I am not able to see it.

_____I listen and validate a person's feelings *before* offering advice.

_____I offer advice in a way that shows I respect the person's feelings and desires. I ask, "Where are you trying to go?" before giving directions.

_____I do not pressure people to do things that they do not want to do, even if I think those things will be good for them. (The exception is if a person has consented to me pushing them in certain ways, such as if I am their therapist or coach. And even in these cases, I respect their boundaries).

_____I do not pressure people to change their personality (ex: to be more outgoing, flexible, organized, etc.), unless they have told me that they want to change and asked for my help.

_____I ask people if they are okay with things, such as changes in plans, rather than assuming that everything will be okay for everyone.

_____I ask permission before touching someone, unless they have told me that it is okay to touch them in certain ways without asking. If someone tells me to stop touching them, I stop. If I am not sure that someone wants me to continue touching them, I stop and check in with them.

_____I am aware of the ways in which I have power and influence over other people, whether through authority, a leadership position, age, or social capital. I am especially consent-conscious when dealing with people who may feel obligated to go along with what I ask, or who know that people would listen to me before listening to them. I avoid pursuing intimate relationships with people I have power over.

_____Everyone is entitled to have negative feelings. I do not push people to have a positive attitude about things that are not positive for them.

_____By validating people's feelings, I make the real world a better place every day.

# Acknowledgements

This book would not have been possible without all of the positive forces in my life.

First, thank you to Eli Dupree for all of your help on this book – your line-by-line edits, as well as your general guidance. I've learned so much from all of your editing advice on this book. You're the best unofficial writing teacher I've ever had. Thank you for your cover design and for letting me include your "How to Be Awesome" letter. But beyond that, thank you for being such a validating friend, for standing by me through everything, and for teaching me what it truly means to be validating and consent-conscious. You taught me that it was okay to want to be treated with a level of validation that I was not being treated with at the time that we met, and you've raised my standards of how we should all be treating each other. You helped me to realize that my feelings are valid, that it's okay to not be okay with things as they are, and that it's okay to want to make things better. Thank you for being my role model of what it means to be a positive force in someone's life.

Thank you to Emily for validating my feelings about college and helping me find the courage to share my truth. Thank you for helping me work out so many parts of the book through our conversations about validation. Talking about validation with you helped me to realize how much I cared about this issue. Every time you told me that you learned something from my story, it made me feel empowered, like I could teach other people as well.

Thank you to Sam for all of your feedback and moral support on this book, and for helping me realize that I was not alone in my beliefs.

Thank you to Nicole, Nabila, and Izzy for all of your moral support, and for being such validating friends.

Thank you to my cousin Aarti for your guidance on the publishing process, and for your moral support.

Thank you to Dr. Jennifer Lish and Jennifer Eaton for all of your support and encouragement. You both helped me to write with emotional honesty again, reclaim my story, and find the courage to share this book with the world.

Finally, thank you to my family for all of your loving support, not just on this book, but on all of my writing throughout my life.

Thank you to Uncle Gary for your legal guidance and moral support on this book. Thank you for always listening to my stories, taking my writing seriously, and believing in me.

Thank you to Auntie Donna for listening to all of my stories and poems when I was growing up, for believing in me, and for always being excited to hear about my new projects.

Thank you to Grandma and Grandpa for all of your unconditional love and support throughout my life. You came to all of my events and cheered me on in everything that I did. You loved listening to my stories and poems, and you read my very first books, taped together with shoebox hardcovers. I wish so much that you could be here to read my first real book. You'll always be at my core, and I'll always be your little lovebug.

And most importantly, thank you to Mom and Dad for all of your unconditional love and support, and for always believing in me. You've both encouraged me in my writing as far back as I can remember. You listened to my stories and ideas for hours and hours on end, and you've always taken my writing seriously and supported my becoming a writer when I grew up. Thank you to Dad for writing down all of my poems when I was younger. I was making them up just for fun, but you wanted to record every single one, and that taught me the value that my writing had. Thank you to Mom for reading so many books with me, and for teaching me how to make pop-up books and making books together with me. You've given me the most feedback on my writing throughout my life. When everyone else would just say that it was good, you gave me specific feedback so that I could improve. Even when I was really young, you would always point out specific details that you liked about my stories and poems. You treated them just like any published works. Thank you for all of the feedback and editing help that you gave me on this book. Thank you both for always being there for me no matter what. Your unconditional love made me who I am today.

94345145R00133

Made in the USA
Middletown, DE
19 October 2018